ABOUT THE AUTHOR

Arthur Milton has built an enviable reputation since February 1945, when he established The Arthur Milton Organization. The organization offers expertise in every area of insurance and financial matters. Hundreds of thousands have been privy to the Milton concepts, which have strengthened their financial security.

As an author, his teachings on economic subjects have been read by millions of Americans, who have benefited from his sage and honest advice. *How Your Life Insurance Policies Rob You*, his most recent book, has revolutionized the staid life insurance industry for the benefit of all consumers.

A Nation Saved: Thank You, President Reagan is Arthur Milton's twelfth published book. He admits that this one was inspired by his feeling of gratitude towards the present administration for what he believes it has done to reverse the downward trend that America has been on for the past thirty-five years.

Mr. Milton lives and works in his native New York City and currently serves as National Chairman of the Citizens Committee for the United States Mission to the United Nations. He is a member of The President's Committee.

A NATION SAVED ☆ ☆ ☆

Thank You, President Reagan

by ARTHUR MILTON

CITADEL PRESS ☆ SECAUCUS, NEW JERSEY

Published by Citadel Press
A division of Lyle Stuart Inc.
120 Enterprise Avenue, Secaucus, N.J. 07094
In Canada by Musson Book Company
A division of General Publishing Co. Limited
Don Mills, Ontario

Queries regarding rights and permissions should be
addressed to: Lyle Stuart Inc., 120 Enterprise Avenue,
Secaucus, N.J. 07094

Manufactured in the United States of America

Library of Congress Cataloging in Publication Data

Milton, Arthur, 1922-
   A nation saved.

   1. United States—Economic policy—1981-
2. United States—Politics and government—1981-
3. Reagan, Ronald.   I. Title.
HC106.8.M56   1983   338.973   83-7604
ISBN 0-8065-0870-1

Dedication

I dedicate this book to the founding fathers of our country, who created the world's first government of the people, by the people and for the people.

They established the freedoms which laid the foundations of our society, freedom of conscience, freedom of speech, freedom of opportunity and freedom from fear. Out of these grew The Free Enterprise System which Ronald Reagan is so determined to restore and preserve, in order to provide for the needs as well as the wants of all Americans.

Also to the tens of millions who will realize there is nothing free in life, and who know that they must hold their heads high and regain their self-respect and become self-reliant under the principles of our great country.

Acknowledgments

I am so grateful to the thousands of people of the A.L. Williams Organization I met in 1982. Their inspiration and dedication for what is right in America led me to embark on the writing of this book.

To them I owe a debt of gratitude for their friendship and companionship as I went from coast to coast and border to border re-acquainting myself with everything that makes our country so great.

They in their own way have helped me spread the gospel of the free American enterprise system in righting the wrongs for 231 million Americans by speaking out the truth on insurance and financial matters.

* * *

To my friend of a quarter of a century, Leroy Pope of United Press International fame, I thank him for teaching me so much about the America we all love.

* * *

To Anthony S. Faillace, Jr., with much gratitude for his help and encouragement as I proceeded in my efforts to expound on my thoughts about the man, Ronald Reagan.

Contents

Introduction

President Reagan wisely put victory over inflation and high interest rates ahead of full employment as the primary goal in restoring the United States to social and economic health. The alternative is utter destruction of everything our forefathers have built in the past three hundred years. In spite of the fact that agriculture has ceased to be a big employer of labor, manufacturing may follow the same course. The unemployment problem is not as great as it seems to be to those who are jobless, and the Reagan program is, in the long run, the best hope for creating new jobs.

PART ONE

The Leader

A collection of interviews with prominent personalities giving their opinions of Ronald Reagan's character and of the achievements of his first years in the White House.

PART TWO

America's Greatest Hour of Trial

Getting inflation down to annual rate of 1.5 percent for several months in a row was a great victory, but consolidating the victory will be hard. There inevitably will be casualties. Thirty-five years of folly can't be overcome in four years. The twenty-four critical problems that must be solved.

decisions. The need for more transactional and consumption taxes. The flat tax schemes. Tax shelter abuses and abuses of Social Security taxes. Excessive professionalism in politics keeps taxes wastefully high.

Big government and high taxes have driven up to 30 percent of the national economy underground in order to evade taxes and government regulation. The same thing is happening all over the world. The existence of the underground economy makes government statistics incomplete, giving us a totally false picture of what's going on in the country. Politicians ignore the underground economy, so eventually it could paralyze the government and erode all social values.

Crime is the fifth horseman of the Apocalypse. It has increased more in the past twenty-five years than in 325 years previously. It costs us $150 billion a year but the greater cost is in human misery, degradation and frustration. The ultimate cause of crime is not known. Some of the many things wrong with our police and courts, how lawyers profit off crime and cause it to spread and increase.

Many economists and other experts now are convinced that the western free enterprise nations are losing their ability to compete in the world because they have become hopelessly extravagant welfare states. The Third World countries have avoided this trap. The communist countries are welfare states but they are extremely austere. Nobody can live in the modern world without exporting, and if we can't compete we could perish.

The scandalous failings of the U.S. housing industry. No rental housing or affordable homes to buy for the working classes. How this makes it difficult to run or create a business or to manage a community. Our economic policies make it safer and more profitable to speculate in old housing than to build new housing. Inflation and high interest rates have diverted capital from needed housing construction.

Conclusion 210

We must stop putting our efforts and capital into such wasteful enterprises as gambling, pornography, extravagant professional and college sporting attractions, such frippery as videogames, consumer credit card excesses and (wasteful) profligate advertising. Inflation and high interest rates have brought our farmers to the edge of bankruptcy and the brink of rebellion and this could threaten food production. We must curb corruption, laziness and sloth and unthinking arrogance on the part of many elements of our society. President Reagan's breaking the Air Traffic Controllers strike was a turning point in the right direction.

A NATION SAVED
Thank You, President Reagan

Introduction

A TREMENDOUS DEBATE is raging over which of two great evils plaguing American society must be dealt with first—inflation, accompanied by record high interest rates, or unemployment.

Naturally many of those out of work, young persons just entering the labor market and millions who simply are devoted to liberal and radical convictions, think first attention must be given to providing jobs. They believe passionately that inflation and high interest rates are the result of monetary mismanagement and other inefficiencies on the part of the government and business, and of selfishness on the part of the rich. Therefore they insist jobs can be created for all, inflation can be kept under control and interest rates brought down, all at the same time.

Many of these people tend to believe that this is being accomplished in the communist world. It isn't. The communist societies all have inflation, a high cost of money, and unemployment to deal with, although not in precisely the same ways as the western nations. If they didn't, they would not have to maintain such tight controls on their economies. The enormously excessive police power of the state in communist countries enables them to conceal the extent of inflation and unemployment, and to squelch any large-scale public protests over either.

Those Americans—a growing majority in all likelihood—who believe in keeping a permanent lid on infla-

11

tion and getting rid of high interest rates, giving them top priority over providing jobs, also believe that, in the long run, their ideas will result in much greater and more natural growth of employment than any make-work program or easy-money program that tolerates renewed inflation.

In simplest terms, this growing majority favors most of President Reagan's economic principles and believes the return to double digit inflation and prolonged high interest rates can utterly wreck the American economy and erode the entire fabric of American society. We know cyclical unemployment cannot do that because we have survived some periods of cyclical unemployment in the past that were worse than we have now—the first half of the 1930s for example.

We cannot gloss over the fact that unemployment probably is going to be harder to solve now than it was following the other recessions since World War II. Many industries, including the automobile industry, the kingpin of the national economy ever since Henry Fords's marvelous model T car first appeared, now are becoming less important to the nation in terms of jobs. Key industries are ceasing to be big employers altogether. Agriculture is in many respects still our most important activity. It feeds all of us and it provides the biggest chunk of our export trade, but farming now is so mechanized and automated that it accounts for less than 5 percent of our labor force. Sixty years ago it was the biggest employer. Not surprisingly it has the lowest unemployment rate of any industry, less than 2 percent.

What is really troubling is that manufacturing, the big employer of blue collar workers, seems clearly to be going the way of agriculture and will cease to be a major employer. We should not be surprised at that. The late Professor Norbert Wiener of Massachusetts Institute of Technology, author of the popular book *Cybernetics*, predicted it twenty-five years or more ago.

Already white collar jobs outnumber blue collar jobs in America by a margin of five to three and high technology industries and service industries, plus retailing and wholesaling, are more important employers than the old basic industries.

This suggests that not only is trying to solve unemployment less urgent than controlling inflation and interest rates, but that it cannot be done simply with infusions of tax money, as many of the jobless and their political sympathizers believe.

Also, the unemployment situation does not look anywhere as bad, as a national problem, as it does to individuals enduring the anguish and frustration of not having a job. Everyone knows that officially recorded unemployment hit a record level since World War II of over 10 percent in late 1982, and that figure was low because some jobless persons had become too discouraged to continue to register.

Nevertheless, this figure also deceived most Americans into thinking unemployment is worse than it really is because they tend to get their information mainly from skimpy television and radio broadcasts rather than from the more complete accounts in the daily newspapers and more authoritative magazines. Here are some important facts about the current level of unemployment that most Americans never find out.*

—Forty percent of all the jobless have not been laid off. They quit their last jobs voluntarily and are just entering or re-entering the labor market.
—While a significant proportion of the jobless remain out of work for long periods, most do not. The median period of unemployment is eight and a half weeks and nearly 40 percent find a new job in four weeks.
—The unemployment level for married males was only 6 percent when the general level hit over 10 percent.
—About one-sixth of those registered as unemployed are not looking for full-time jobs. They only want part-time work.
—While many unemployed are destitute or on welfare, the Census Bureau said in its April, 1982, *Monthly Labor Review* that about half of all families with one or more members unemployed still have aggregate incomes of $20,000 a year or more.

*Fortune Magazine, June 14, 1982, p. 64.

Also, as I show in Chapter 7, the official figures on unemployment are exaggerated because they do not take into
account the very substantial number of persons working
either full-time or part-time in the underground economy.
Millions of these people are listed as unemployed yet are
working bringing home the bacon every week.

Just how much the official unemployment rate is distorted is not subject to scientifical statistical proof, but it is
very substantial.

Nevertheless, certain aspects of the unemployment
mess are every bit as bad as they appear to be—unemployment among black teenagers, for example. Mechanization
of farming in the South, which started in the 1950s, is a big
cause of this, according to Assistant Secretary of Labor
John Cogan. Both Cogan and Professor Walter E. Williams
of George Mason University in Virginia, an eminent black
economist, say the federal minimum wage law, a darling of
the AFL-CIO and liberal politicians, is much to blame for
keeping black teenagers idle. Cogan and Williams contend
that employers would hire substantially more black teenagers if the minimum wage law were repealed and that it
would be better for the youngsters to work at lower wages
than to be idle and perhaps drift into crime. Of course,
some do work at less than the legal minimum wage in the
underground economy.

If we conclude then that priority must be given to keeping the lid on inflation and reducing interest rates, how do
we go about accomplishing that?

We have discovered in recent years that increasing the
money supply no longer will bring interest rates down automatically, as it would years ago, because it just spurs inflation in today's economic climate.

That's what this book is about.

I wrote a book instead of just an article or a pamphlet
because it's a very difficult subject. It deals with some
rather simple truths, but simple truths often are the hardest
to get people to accept.

Fortune magazine set out recently to prove that compel-
ling the Federal Reserve System to hold the growth of the
money supply down to 1.5 percent a year would be the best

way to bring interest rates down, because that would calm virtually all fears of renewed inflation. *Fortune* contended that when interest rates reach a level of 15 percent, that means that the real interest rate due to national economic causes is about 9 percent; the remaining 6 percent is caused entirely by fear of renewed inflation. But the article conceded that the public sees things differently. It said that the public believes that inflation and resulting high interest rates are caused almost entirely by federal deficit spending.

My inclination is to agree with the public. But you and I and all the rest of the public must face up to the fact that we actually *are* responsible for the deficit spending. We permit it. We elect the politicians who appoint the bureaucrats who do the spending. We demand much of the spending with strident voices, pressure blocs and expensive lobbies.

Each one of us wants the most economical government services for everybody else, but our attitude usually is that any public extravagance is okay if it benefits me and my family and my business. That attitude is what we must put a stop to.

The first part of the book is devoted to some impressions of Ronald Reagan and his views on this engrossing problem by some of his close associates who were kind enough to talk to me and give me the benefit of their experiences with Mr. Reagan as governor of California and in the White House.

Little did I realize as a boy learning geography and history during the Great Depression that I would be privileged some fifty years later to sit with those in high-level positions of our government and discuss the issues that led me to write this book.

ARTHUR MILTON

PART ONE

The Leader

MOST BOOKS that assess the state of the nation are written by politicians or professors. Journalists turn out a few. Not many are done by businessmen.

The politicians have one of two aims. If they have come to the end of the road in office or plainly are in the twilight of their careers, they frankly are out to merchandise their reminiscences. Any effort to describe current affairs, interpret the past or foresee the future is likely to be perfunctory and subordinated to condoning the author's own mistakes in office and to paying off old scores.

If the politician is writing while still young and active, it's a safe bet that the book will in effect ride a pet hobbyhorse and press a scheme or idea that hopefully will lead to a step up the political ladder or at least to reelection.

The motives of the academic authors are more varied. The professors are compulsive, if frequently dull, writers because the most important dictum in the American academic world is "publish or perish." A mere teacher is doomed to be a drudge for life even though such a career may be of infinitely more value to the youth of the land and to society in general than those of the ambitious scholars who spew out books in order to keep their names before the lords of the academic Establishment.

Of course, a professor can satisfy the "publish or perish law" by writing about his or her own specialty, whether that be ancient Greek history or one of the more abstruse areas of mathematics or microbiology; but to win a really wide readership and resulting public attention, the aspiring scholar must bring his personality to bear on a subject of vast public interest. If expertise in one's own academic discipline is germane to an area of public affairs, that's fine. But even if it isn't, no matter—anybody can be an ideologue. That's why we have professors of languages, psychology, physics, or organic chemistry writing books that confidently tell us how to solve the nation's fiscal, political and criminal ills.

The books done by the academic ideologues in obedience to the "publish or perish law" are virtually all research works, done in an atmosphere that businessmen and ordinary folk describe as "ivory tower." These works seldom derive from personal experience or contacts. Of course, the research may be extremely well done and the academic authors quite often are excellent thinkers. After all, they didn't get their Ph.D's and their tenured posts without a lot of hard and conscientious toil.

The businessman keeps up with what's going on in the world as everyone else does by keeping his eyes and ears open, but he does not have the time for detailed and systemized research. The successful businessman learns over and over again that theory without practice is impractical. He turns to writing for just one reason, because he likes to write; and although he may hire someone to do some research for him, he soon finds that studying the research reports is almost as tedious as doing the research itself. So he writes mainly from his convictions, and he quickly realizes that the ideas and feelings he wants to put on paper grow out of his contacts with people. He discovers that he must talk with more people who know more than he does about the matter in hand because they are closer to it and are engaged every day in coping with the situation and the problems it causes.

That is why I decided to nose about in Washington and interview people who know Ronald Reagan and work for him and with him. (To have had the opportunity to walk through the halls of our White House and other of our government institutions is something I wish every American could experience.) The interviews in Part I of this book are the results of that decision. They reflect a cross-section of opinions from the hundreds of people in and out of government that I was privileged to talk with.

Helene Von Damm in her office at the White House telling me all about that man, Ronald Reagan.

Helene Von Damm

IT IS POSSIBLE that no one except his wife, Nancy, knows Ronald Reagan's ideas and principles better than Helene Von Damm, his former White House deputy and now ambassador to Austria.

She was his personal secretary during seven of his eight years as governor of California. She had quit a good job at the political action committee of the American Medical Association in Chicago to go to California and work for his campaign organization after meeting him and hearing his message.

"What he had to say struck a nerve and it changed my life," the petite Austrian-born Ms. Von Damm told me in her office at the White House.

Just why did the candidacy of a film and television actor for the governorship of a state half a continent away mean so much in 1965 to a chic young woman who had worked her way up from a typist in a Detroit insurance office to a responsible political post for one of the country's most important professional societies?

21

"I'll tell you why," she told me. "It's because, unlike native Americans, I grew up under the grim rule of the occupying communist Russian army. I experienced communism!"

She grew up during World War II, living in a small Austrian town with her parents and brother, took a course as a stenographer and secretary in a provincial business school, then went to Vienna to find a decent job.

"I was curious and in search of a better life when I determined to see some of the world."

She spent two years in Sweden and Germany where she met and married her first husband, an American, who brought her to the United States. Her first home was Detroit, where she developed an intense interest in the political institutions and climate in America that we natives take so much for granted that we rarely study them or even think about them. It was Ronald Reagan's passionate defense of the ideals of Washington, Jefferson and Lincoln that drew Helene to San Francisco to work in his campaign.

"Then I got lucky," she explained. Reagan's cabinet secretary Bill Clark asked her to go to Sacramento and within a year she became the governor's personal secretary.

As the president's assistant for presidental personnel, Ms. Von Damm's duties were numerous and significant, but the reason I sought an interview with her is that for seventeen years she had access to virtually all of Ronald Reagan's voluminous correspondence, both official and personal. She could answer questions about the president's life and his views and convictions more quickly and more accurately than anyone I could think of. I could take it for granted that she believed his first two years in the White House were a real turning point in our history because she believed that his first active appearance on the political horizon seventeen years ago was a prophetic turning point.

She also believes that Mr. Reagan will run for reelection in 1984. But she recalled that he had steadfastly refused to seek a third term as governor of California although the general feeling was that he could have won again easily.

She also recalled that, in a letter to R.G. Friedman of Fort Lauderdale, Florida, in 1975, Reagan said the United States needs more than anything a one-term president who will take on all the problems with no thought of the next election.

Now, that statement did not say a president should not accept renomination if it is offered to him. It did say he should not actually seek renomination and should not let thoughts about renomination influence any of his policies.

About the same time, Ms. Von Damm said, Reagan told many of his friends that he had "the old-fashioned belief that the office should seek the man. . . . A man should not run for president as an ego trip. There should be a legitimate and significant demand for his leadership from the public."

She also told me that Ronald Reagan said very soberly that he never had sought the governorship but rather was drafted into the office and that he took it at a considerable financial sacrifice. He was making about five times as much as a film and TV actor as the governorship paid in salary.

When I asked her what she considered the most important single characteristic of Ronald Reagan, the public man, she said it is the fact that, ever since he first ran for governor, he has described himself as a "citizen politician," not a professional politician. She said he explained frequently that this means "that I made a pledge to myself that I would make every decision on the basis that I would never run for office again. It didn't mean that I wouldn't run again, but I felt that the first time a man in public office makes a decision on the basis of what it might do or might not do with regard to votes in the next election, he has begun the path of compromise from which there is no turning back." Reagan wrote this in answer to a letter from a lady in Texas who told him bluntly that, since he was a politician, she couldn't give him her unqualified support.

Let us consider the full meaning of what Ms. Von Damm told me. It appears to mean that Ronald Reagan doesn't believe politics can be a career in the way any ordinary occupation can be. We, all of us, know that to hold our jobs and bring home a paycheck we have to bow to the boss's authority and accommodate ourselves to his views and decisions even if they are not as wise or scrupulous as we would like. In fact, the boss must step fairly far out of line before we will give up the paycheck. So long as all that is at stake is an individual's personal economic welfare, that's a reasonable attitude. But for the political executive or legislator who must make decisions involving the lives, liberties and welfare of millions, Ronald Reagan says it isn't enough.

In her 1976 book *Sincerely, Ronald Reagan,* based entirely on Reagan's correspondence, Helene Von Damm has a whole chapter on this concept of the citizen politician. She recounts that Governor Reagan told members of his staff, "We belong here only so long as we refer to the government as *'they'* and never think of the government as *'we.'"*

She explained to me that, as a citizen politician, Reagan would not take stands on public issues—local, national or international—just to make himself popular. She cited many examples of his refusal to compromise for the sake of popularity, and to my mind whether Reagan was right or wrong in his stand on each issue is far less important than the fact that in a poltical career of seventeen years he has kept the courage to refuse to bow to personal political expediency.

Ms. Von Damm also reminded me that in his November, 1975, announcement that he would run against President Ford for the Republican presidential nomination, Reagan revealed one of his more important reasons for deserting the Democratic Party after having been for years a fervant Roosevelt New Dealer. She said Mr. Reagan declared in this announcement speech that the Democratic Party had ignored a solemn warning by Roosevelt himself of the dangers for the nation that the New Deal had created. Reagan said that FDR "embarked on a course that made bold use of government to ease the pain [of hard times]" and that "although some of these measures seemed to work, he soon was moved to utter a warning—'we have built up new instruments of public power in the hands of the people's government . . . but in the hands of political puppets of an economic autocracy, such power could provide shackles for the liberties of the people.' " FDR's warning on excessive powers has guided Reagan's career.

"Unfortunately his [FDR's] warning went unheeded. Today there is an economic autocracy because of government interference in the control of the economy. . . . Over these past four decades political puppets of this autocracy have persuaded first one group, then another to turn to government for answers to problems it was never designed to solve."

We think of autocracy as concentration of power, but it is more than that; it is self-perpetuating concentration of power in the hands of one element of society. It can be an aristocratic autocracy, a socialist or communist autocracy, a military or religious autocracy or a bureaucratic autocracy such as we now have in this country that makes mere puppets of most of our elected officials.

We will see later on in this book, in the chapter on the underground economy, just how farsighted FDR was in his warning. Many thoughtful observers around the world believe the growth of big government and the rise of excessive professionalism in politics really have made two-dimensional puppets out of politicians instead of well-rounded, responsible people capable of independent thought and decisions.

Ms. Von Damm also said Reagan's letters frequently declared that the Democratic Party had abandoned the principles of Jefferson and Jackson.

Politics frequently has been defined as the art of the possible, and that definition implies that politics thus is the art of compromise. If we apply Ronald Reagan's concept of the citizen politician as a test to this definition, it immediately becomes apparent that politics is the art of honest and decent compromise—never of surrender.

Ms. Von Damm of course was proud of Reagan's achievement in curbing inflation and expressed the hope that the drop in interest rates that began in the autumn of 1982 would continue. She recalled that he was among the very first political leaders in America to try to do something constructive about inflation and high taxes. As governor he proposed a fifteen-year program to gradually reduce California's income tax by 20 percent. In a letter to the Rev. David Ellingson in 1974 he wrote, "This country must take the lead in controlling the cost of government, which leads to inflation, and stop this runaway increase in prices as well as the enormous tax burdens being borne by the people." Reagan declared in a letter to a California voter back in 1972, "The plain truth is that for many, many years we have all been lied to about taxing business and thus reducing the individual's tax burden. There is no way that business can be made to pay tax. Business collects taxes and if businesses cannot include all their taxes as production expenses in the prices of their products, they go out of business. There are one hundred and sixteen business taxes, so-called, in the price of a suit of clothes. All these taxes are passed on to the ultimate consumer, the individual citizen. The real problem with taxes in our country is simply the high cost of government and taxes cannot be lowered until people hold government more accountable."

Ms. Von Damm spoke to me about the president's views on communism, Soviet aggression, the Middle East and many other matters that are constantly in the news, but we can read about those views of Ronald Reagan every day. Much more interesting were her observations and recollections about his personal, moral and philosophical convictions and his enthusiasms. She spoke about his love for the outdoors, his fondness for horses and cattle, his liking for swimming, his life-long love affairs with football and the theatre and the movies. The things that impressed her about Ronald Reagan the actor, were his generous praise of other actors and his deep distress over the "new realism" in films with so much resulting explicit sex and brutal violence. "He is not only disgusted at the brutality and depravity," she explained, "he is deeply chagrined because he thinks it is all bad, dull theatre. He says good theatre depends on making everyone in the audience use his or her imagination and that all this four-letter word vulgarity, over-explicit sex, nudism and stultifyingly excessive violence deprives the audience of the privilege of using imagination and thus destroys the magic the old family movies had." She said he is quite free of professional jealousy, although he admitted he almost hated George C. Scott for his great performance in the film *Patton,* a role Reagan very much wanted and didn't get.

Many men in politics give the clear impression that they go to church only because it is the thing to do, but Helene Von Damm says Ronald Reagan is genuinely and deeply religious. She told me he also is a highly moral, sensitive and perceptive man and a kindly man, but is rather stern and orthodox in his religious views, particularly on such controversial issues as abortion. She gave me an example of his orthodoxy: "He said rather simply that since Jesus said 'I am the son of God,' then 'we must believe him or we assume that he was the greatest liar who ever lived.' " And, she said, Reagan asked how a lying charlatan could have had the impact on the world for two thousand years that Jesus has had.

She told me that Mr. Reagan doesn't believe any nation can legislate morality but that he is deeply concerned about the hedonism that humanist philosophy has spread in American society, and is resolute in his conviction that only a rebirth of spirituality and rededication to our traditional moral precepts can solve the nation's greatest problems. He thinks, for example, that is the only way we will ever wipe out the drug traffic and narcotic addiction, or the increase in crime.

She said that perhaps one of the most striking things about Ronald Reagan is that no matter how much he grows in knowledge, his personality and character do not appear to change. She said he has even declared that he doesn't believe a mature adult will or should change much as the years go by because he or she will have acquired attitudes and traits fairly early which are essentially true and sound, and will continue to live by these standards.

At the United States Mission in New York City, Ambassador to the United Nations Jeane Kirkpatrick discusses our world involvements.

Jeane Kirkpatrick

I SOUGHT AN INTERVIEW with Jeane Kirkpatrick, Ronald Reagan's ambassador to the United Nations, for a very different reason.

Unlike Helene Von Damm, Ms. Kirkpatrick is a university professor and has been actively writing about politics for some time with a constituency of her own. Moreover, she was appointed to the vital post at the UN by a Republican president in spite of the fact that she is a registered Democrat. But the most important thing I wanted from Ms. Kirkpatrick was an authoritative estimate of Ronald Reagan's grasp of foreign affairs and how she believes the rest of the world looks at him. I asked her if, in her opinion, the downslide of world opinion of the United States that was so steady during the Carter administration had been stemmed in Ronald Reagan's first two years in the White House, and if we are on the way back in world esteem.

"You must remember," she answered, "that I am a university professor and I get very uncomfortable talking about opinion in the absence of evidence about the opinion, but I think several things could be said. One is that President Carter certainly was not very popular among Europeans. He did not really enjoy the esteem of European leaders. That also was the case when Ronald Reagan first became president, that the worst must be expected of him. For example, I remember being in France when they showed on television that movie *Breakfast with Bonzo* and, particularly, the playing of the scene of Bonzo the ape and a young Ronald Reagan out on a window ledge and engaged in various other perilous adventures. All this was by way of suggesting that Ronald Reagan was not a serious man and would not make a serious president. Certainly I think our European friends learned very quickly that this estimate of President Reagan was a mistake. They learned that he is indeed a serious man who came to meetings with them well prepared and well informed, and generally they liked him."

Ms. Kirkpatrick added that one of Mr. Reagan's personal triumphs in this respect was at the Cancun summit meeting in Mexico held to find ways for the developed nations to help stimulate economic growth and improvement in the developing countries. No really big steps were expected at Cancun but Ms. Kirkpatrick told me: "President Reagan made a very positive impression there on the leaders of both the developed and developing countries, and since then I think he has continued to win their esteem and respect."

Then she added with cautious understatement, "That does not mean that they always agree with him. In fact, from time to time he has made decisions and adopted policies which were not welcome to some of our European allies, the sanctions on that Soviet natural gas pipeline for example. And from time to time he has adopted a policy which he thought was the right thing and has stuck to it regardless of disapproval, but again I think he has stimulated some good healthy respect from our opposite numbers in the world."

I asked her if one reason for that wasn't that Ronald Reagan does not backtrack once he has made a decision as his predecessor did, and if this same forthrightness and constancy had not won some renewed respect for the United States at the United Nations headquarters.

She replied that she believed that, at the UN, it now is generally understood that the Reagan administration is earnest and serious—"not only do we say what we mean, but, more importantly, we mean what we say, that, mainly, when we take positions on issues we will not change our minds next week and we also will stand firmly for the defense of our national interest, our good name and our reputation. We also will stand very firmly for those principles such as human rights and fair play and those laws we think are basically important."

To give me a more comprehensive idea of what she meant, Ms. Kirkpatrick gave me a copy of her 1982 book *Dictators and Double Standards*. The book is a distillation of some of her notable lectures and essays over the past twenty years. It also is somewhat argumentative. She attacks three corrosive and destructive intellectual and political delusions that she thinks have worked havoc in the world through their pernicious impact on international and domestic politics. These delusions are rationalism, utopianism and moralism.

Rationalism gets her special scorn. She says the rationalists, who include most political liberals, simply refuse to face up to what human beings have been in the past, are now and probably will be in the future. They assume falsely that man and society can be brought to conform to a preferred plan and tend to see everything as possible and prospects for progress as unlimited. "When we forget, or wilfully choose to ignore, the intractability of human behavior, the complexity of human institutions, and the probability of unanticipated consequences, we do so at great risk and often immense human cost," she wrote. She told me how she believed American policy under President Carter failed in Iran and Nicaragua.

She said that "even though Iran was rich, blessed with a product the United States and its allies needed badly, and led by a handsome king, while Nicaragua was poor and rocked along under a long-tenure president of less striking aspect, there were many similarities between the two countries and our relations with them. Both these small nations were led by men who had not been selected by free elections, who recognized no duty to submit themselves to searching tests of popular acceptability."

"But," she continued, "both did tolerate opposition newspapers and political parties. However, both were confronted by radical, violent opponents bent on social and political revolution. They both, therefore, sometimes invoked martial law to arrest, imprison, exile and occasionally, it was alleged, torture their opponents. Both relied for public order on police forces whose personnel were said to be too harsh, too arbitrary and too powerful. Each had what the American press termed 'private armies,' which is to say armies pledging their allegiance to the ruler rather than the 'constitution' or 'the nation' or some other impersonal entity."

"In short," she concluded, "both Somoza and the Shah were traditional rulers of semi-traditional societies. Although the Shah very badly wanted to create a technologically modern and powerful nation and Somoza tried hard to introduce modern agricultural methods, neither sought to reform his society in the light of any abstract idea of social justice or political virtue. Neither attempted to alter significantly the distribution of goods, status or power."

"The big thing to remember," she said, "is that the Shah and Somoza not only were anti-communist, sending their sons and others to be educated in our universities, voting with us in the United Nations and regularly supporting American interests and positions even when these entailed personal and political 'sacrifice,' but that each of the two rulers was from time to time criticized by American officials for violating civil and human rights. But the fact that the peoples of Iran and Nicaragua only intermittently enjoyed the rights accorded to citizens in the western democracies did not prevent successive Washington administrations from granting them both military and economic aid. Tangible and intangible tokens of American support continued until these regimes became the objects of a major coup by forces explicitly hostile to the United States."

"But once an attack was launched by opponents bent on destruction, everything changed," she said. "The rise of violent opposition in Iran and Nicaragua set in motion a succession of events which bore a suggestive resemblance to one another and a suggestive similarity to our behavior in China before the fall of Chiang Kai-shek, in Cuba before the triumph of Castro, in certain crucial periods of the Vietnam war, and more recently in Angola."

"The final result," she said, "was that in each of the countries, the American effort to impose liberalization and democratization on a government confronted with violent internal opposition not only failed, but actually assisted the coming to power of new regimes in which ordinary people enjoy fewer freedoms and less personal security than under the previous autocracy—regimes moreover hostile to American interests and policies."

In her book, Ms. Kirkpatrick provides a swift analysis of how the Marxist presence and the supplies of Marxist weapons to rebels in so many countries was minimized or ignored by American officials because the liberal elements in the United States said, "U.S. support for the dictator gives the rebels little choice but to seek aid 'elsewhere.' " She describes the step-by-step buildup of the revolutionary effort, the steady loss of confidence by Washington in the reliability of its traditionalist authoritarian allies, and the invariably abortive efforts to replace the friendly dictators with moderate governments "before it is too late." But even if a moderate government is put in power by popular elections, it almost invariably soon becomes obvious that the moderates lack the political power base or the will to resist the radical revolutionists who are bent on destruction and are backed by the communists. Either the Marxists take over or the rightist military junta, probably led by a fanatic, then seizes power. Ms. Kirkpatrick goes on:

> In either case, the United States will have been led by its own misunderstanding of the situation to assist actively in deposing an erstwhile friend and installing a government hostile to American interests and policies in the world. At best we will have lost access to friendly territory. At worst, the Soviets will have gained a new base. And everywhere our friends will have noted that the United States cannot be

counted on in times of difficulty and our enemies will have observed that American support provides no security.

Reading this passage, one becomes better able to understand why the Reagan administration is taking such a firm line with the pro-Marxist Sandinista regime now in power in Nicaragua and why it continues the struggle in El Salvador for a non-revolutionary solution.

Ms. Kirkpatrick's book is remarkable for the detailed description she gives of how individual American statesmen fell into the fatal trap she described, often in spite of the best intentions possible.

She makes the point several times that the rationalizationists and moralizers in America, particularly those in high posts in the Carter administration, were so naïve that they believed a moderate, liberal government would survive in Iran when the Shah was overthrown and would give the Iranians more freedoms and better economic conditions than the Shah had. Many of them were shocked when the Ayatollah Khomeini and the other bigoted reactionary mullahs overthrew the Bahktiar regime and proceeded to set up a medieval theocracy after a prolonged bloodbath. The rationalizers had showed the same naïveté about the Marxists in Cuba.

She insists that the rationalizationists never learn from the repetition in many corners of the world of this kind of tragedy.

I also asked Ms. Kirkpatrick if the Reagan administration's strong stand at the UN in support of Israel's continued participation in the General Assembly in spite of the differences the president was having with Prime Minister Begin was not further proof that the United States means business.

"Well, I hope so," she replied. "We did mean business, and the fact is that we took our position, not just because we felt the attack on Israel was improper but because that kind of treatment of Israel would have been a clear-cut violation of principle and of the charter on which the United Nations was built. We refuse absolutely to support here any policies that are a violation of the charter of the UN or the Constitution of the United States."

When I asked her about our government's challenging

the Russians by telling them we have positive evidence
that they are using germ warfare and about everything else
in several parts of the world, I added an inquiry as to how
we might ever be able to live with any agreement we
might get with the Russians.

"Well," she answered, "we know that the Soviets indeed
are engaged in the use of chemical weapons—yellow rain
to be specific—in Afghanistan, in Cambodia and certain
other places. We also know that this is a violation of the
Soviet Union's own commitments not to use such weapons.
Their signature to the treaty that bars these weapons
means they have violated their given word. What does that
mean to us? It doesn't mean that we will cease our efforts
to get new agreements concerning arms control and weapons and so forth. However, it does mean we are going to be
very interested in those agreements in verification procedures because we know from experience with the Soviets
that you can't necessarily rely automatically on their
word."

I had no luck in getting her to talk about economics. She
said "I don't know anything about economics and I know
even less about Reaganomics."

But when I asked her to comment on whether Mr.
Reagan had set the sails for the nation's course in the future, she said: "Well, I think that at the time of President
Reagan's election we were at the end of some historic
trends. I think, for example, it was quite clear that continu-
ation of the habit, and it had become a habit, of simply
turning to the federal government for the answers to almost
all questions was no longer feasible and the government
had become as much the problem as the solution—even
more the problem than the solution. The kinds of programs
that were started to solve problems were themselves creating problems."

"And I think," she added, "that Ronald Reagan became
president at a time when American withdrawal and retreat
in international affairs following the Vietnam war had
reached a point that was quite destructive. It was time for
some new approach by the administration. I also think we
were reaching the point where inflation was affecting vir-

tually every family. We know that what we were doing was not working. It was time to try something different. We have done that and now, of course, inflation has come down and the president has gone to work on the unemployment problem and I have no doubt he will make substantial progress on it."

Asked about how many of the unemployed are working in the underground economy, she said she didn't know but that everybody in the government feels that too many persons in the country are out of work. She also said she simply does not know how Ronald Reagan feels about running for reelection in 1984.

When I asked her if she considered Mr. Reagan an unusual president, she replied—"First of all, I like him very much as a person. Second, I do believe and have written my approval of his background. His background is proven both as a Democrat and as a Republican, and as a labor leader, six times elected president of his own union, the Screen Actors Guild. He also had experience as an employer and in political evolution. He has studied the evolution of many other great people in other parts of our society. All this made him particularly well suited to express himself, to understand and confront some of the kinds of problems that the country faces today, both domestic and international."

With Secretary of Labor Raymond J. Donovan at the Labor Department in Washington, D.C.

Raymond J. Donovan

RAYMOND J. DONOVAN, our sometimes controversial secretary of labor, told me that when the going got tough for him, as it did for some months, he took comfort in the fact that he is serving "a man who in my view will go down in history as the president who saved our way of life."

"We can all remember," he said, "that when we were young we constantly saw in print or heard on the air waves the proud statement that 'only in America' could such and such wonderful thing happen. We haven't been hearing that for some years now, but Ronald Reagan's basic intuition into what is good for Americans will make us again start hearing the proud statement 'only in America—' "

Donovan insisted that, contrary to what critics say, "Ronald Reagan has kept his promises more than any other president," and that by doing so he ended a situation in which we were on the brink of a major economic catastrophe.

"Would you have believed," he asked me, "that Ronald Reagan could have been so successful in combatting inflation?"

But Donovan doesn't by any means take a naïve or fatuously optimistic view of the present situation, and he said that Reagan did not either. "The president has said," Donovan declared, "that we have traded one misery for another, inflation for unemployment."

He said the president had the courage to make the hard policy choices that will reduce both inflation and unemployment in the long run.

When I asked Secretary Donovan how real the official unemployment figures are and how big he thinks the underground economy is, he answered quite honestly that he didn't know. "I didn't even know until I became secretary of labor that 1.5 million of the persons listed as unemployed are high school teenagers seeking summer jobs, and I don't think one American in a hundred knows that."

He conceded that listing these kids as if they were part of the adult unemployed alters the reality of the statistics.

He also conceded that most people in government and politics are loath to involve themselves in sticky questions such as the size of the underground economy because "it's so hard to come by provable figures and because you sound insensitive to the plight of the jobless if you try to answer questions about the underground economy."

He said he had heard that the underground economy in California alone amounted to $80 billion a year. "I have no real way of knowing, but you hear that figure kicked around," he added.

"We're the most honest people in the world," he told me, but added that years of misuse of public funds, high taxes and inflation have encouraged the underground economy and even forced poeple into it. "When the system gets out of kilter and people feel it is unfair, they will find ways to beat the system."

Donovan isn't a chap to blink and swallow unpleasant truths. He said that not enough notice is taken of the fact that the various jobless trust funds now are $17 billion in

debt to the federal government and this debt is rising towards $25 billion. That leads him to believe there clearly
has been some misuse of these funds.

"I get the feeling sometimes," he said, "that for the element we are talking about [people who abuse unemployment insurance], unemployment compensation is less an
insurance program than a paid vacation program."

Donovan ran a large construction firm in New Jersey before becoming secretary of labor. Early in his working
years he was a member of the Brewery Workers Union and
of the International Brotherhood of Electrical Workers. He
said that in the building industry, which he knows well,
there are workers who refuse work after they have earned a
certain amount for the year because the pay would push
them into a higher income tax bracket. "Instead, they take
a vacation for a month or so in Florida and collect unemployment insurance."

Nevertheless, Donovan considers the present unemployment situation graver than those of the past: "On top of
our cyclical unemployment is our displaced worker problem and this has not yet been addressed. It began to be
serious in the mid-1970s, particularly in the automobile industry, and then spread to others. This displacement of
people by technological change hangs heavy in my heart,"
he said, "and this is going to be the first administration to
really address the problem."

For example, he said, under a new Reagan job training
program, 70 cents of every dollar spent actually will go into
retraining the unemployed. He said that under the Carter
CETA program, only 18 cents of each dollar really went
into retraining.

For that and other reasons, Donovan told me he expects
Ronald Reagan to be remembered as a champion of the
poor even though he is at present being vilified because of
unemployment and the necessary cuts in special programs
to bring the federal deficit down.

"But overall," he said, "Ronald Reagan will be remembered as he wants to be, as the man who turned the country
around."

Here, Secretary of Housing and Urban Development Samuel Riley Pierce, Jr., greets me with a hearty welcome in his Washington, D.C. office.

Samuel Riley Pierce, Jr.

SAMUEL RILEY PIERCE, JR., our secretary of housing and urban development, also told me that President Reagan's policies are averting a prolonged depression. He said that when the president was inaugurated we were headed for a depression worse than that of 1929—"We were taxing and spending ourselves into disaster."

"Now," he said, "the upturn definitely has begun. The housing market is really taking off and, since the housing industry historically has led us out of recession, I am confident that pattern is being borne out again. Any time interest rates go down a point, thousands more American families are able to realize the old dream of home ownership."

Pierce said that when the FHA guaranteed mortgage rate was 17½ percent in August, 1981, fewer than five million American families could afford the $885 monthly charge for a thirty-year $60,000 mortgage."But when I announced a 12 percent FHA rate in October, 1982, that meant 10.5 million families could afford such a mortgage."

Pierce said that, under the Reagan administration, HUD has been able to do other things to bring down the cost of new homes. For example, HUD has sponsored in 23 cities a Joint Venture for Affordable Housing program that cuts building costs through deregulation and streamlined processing. The results are savings of as much as 20%. For example, in Lincoln, Nebraska, a builder has been able through the Joint Venture to put a $40,000 price tag on the same kind of house that is selling for $50,000 in the same area. More ventures like this are being launched around the country.

Pierce is convinced that housing is going to make the nation's economy strong again. He points to the substantial reduction in inflation—from 12.5% in 1980 to under 4% at present—and in interest rates, which have come down from a prime rate of 21.5% in January 1981 to 10.5% today. The combination of housing prices that are no longer escalating wildly and mortgages available at lower rates make home ownership affordable for many more Americans, a fact which is borne out by the recent increase in home sales, housing starts, and related economic indicators. Pierce also mentions that there are some 3,000 individual products which go into a new home—from appliances to paint to furnishings—so industries other than construction are helped by a housing recovery.

To help low- and moderate-income Americans realize the dream of home ownership, Pierce said HUD is emphasizing FHA's traditional role of serving first-time homebuyers and insuring rural and inner-city properties. "We do not intend to compete with private insurers," he said. "Rather, we will target our FHA activities to those who are unserved or underserved in the market.

"At the same time, through FHA and GNMA, we have been encouraging the introduction and use of innovative mortgage instruments to help the homebuyer. These new instruments reflect the need for mortgage instruments other than the standard 25- or 30-year fixed payment mortgage. They include: Shared Equity Mortgages, Graduated Payment Mortgages, and Growing Equity Mortgages."

HUD is also instituting direct endorsement of FHA-insured loans as a better way of serving the "FHA market," i.e., primarily first-time and low- to moderate-income urban homebuyers. Direct endorsement, which is scheduled to begin in early May, is one way of improving FHA's program efficiency.

Pierce is so sure that President Reagan is going in the right direction he told me he doesn't think the continuing high unemployment would hurt his chances if he decided to run again in 1984: "If recovery in other industries begins following the recovery in housing, the actual level of unemployment will not hurt him," he said.

He also told me he doesn't believe Mr. Reagan's age will cut much ice when he makes up his mind whether or not to seek reelection. "He will decide on the basis of how good a job he thinks he has done and how much more good he thinks he can accomplish."

"To me," he concluded, "Ronald Reagan is a tremendous person. I particularly admire his self-discipline, both his physical and his temperamental discipline. I have never seen him lose his temper. He keeps his cool under all circumstances and, in my opinion, he has excellent judgment. And, as everybody knows, he is a tremendous communicator. He's a man of principle—that separates him from a lot of politicians."

At the White House with William P. Clarke, the president's Assistant for National Security Affairs.

Judge William P. Clark

JUDGE WILLIAM P. CLARK, the president's assistant for national security affairs, is ex officio chief executive of the National Security Council, of which the president is chairman.

Judge Clark, who was on the California Supreme Court from 1973 to 1981, is another long-time associate of Ronald Reagan. A graduate of Stanford, he served in the Army Counter Intelligence Corps before entering Loyola Law School in Los Angeles. He became Governor Reagan's cabinet secretary and a member of his task force for government reorganization.

He left the security of California's top court for the somewhat perilous post of deputy to Reagan's first secretary of state, Gen. Alexander Haig, and switched over to the White House in January, 1982. He is considered quite a contrast to the president's first national security chief, Richard V. Allen, who stubbed his toe over failing to report a $1,000 gift for arranging an interview with the First Lady

for a Japanese journalist. Allen was cleared of wrongdoing
but he had made himself look careless. Allen and Haig had
feuded and the public often got the impression that they
both were trying to call the shots on U.S. foreign policy
without bothering to submit the issues in full to Ronald
Reagan and wait for his judgment. Inevitably, this didn't sit
well with the top boss for long, so both Allen and Haig
departed.

Judge Clark clearly is not the man to put himself forward
as a rival to the new secretary of state, George Shultz, or to
give the idea that he is taking Ronald Reagan for granted
because of old friendship. In his first year of running the
National Security Council's staff of one hundred in its
widespread day-to-day operations, which include coordi-
nating intelligence, defense and foreign policy for the
president, Clark has gone a long way toward accomplishing what Dick Allen failed to do. He has proved himself a
tough manager and a skilled organizer of a disciplined
team. He has made it crystal clear to all inside and outside
of government and to the diplomatic community that
Ronald Reagan and only Ronald Reagan calls the shots in
U.S. foreign policy. He has converted the Security Council
staff into an efficient force that transforms the president's
philosophy into policy.

He has done more. He has tightened up the preparations
for and the operations of the Security Council meetings so
that the president gets a prompt and sound assessment of
the views of all his key national security advisers on the
issue at hand, including their recommended courses of
action.

Judge Clark's views on Ronald Reagan and his presidency are known to be these: He considers the president a
leader with the durable qualities of greatness. Even before
the 1980 election, Mr. Reagan offered new hope for the
country. As governor of California, he provided leadership
to that huge state at a crucial moment in history. Clearly,
Judge Clark feels Mr. Reagan also has provided such leadership as president, and that he is proceeding in much the
same way he did as governor, being willing to listen to all
points of view before making a decision. Clark also knows

that Ronald Reagan never ducks a decision, no matter how tough the decision is.

In his rather rare speeches and public comments, Judge Clark has let it be known that he thinks the United States is a lot better off from the point of view of national security than it was two years ago, because the president has moved to restore our military strength as he promised he would. After four years of the Carter administration, friends and allies around the world were starting to wonder if America had any real leaders left or if the United States still was capable of a leading role in the world. As Judge Clark sees it, Ronald Reagan has changed all that because his leadership has given us back our self-confidence and self-respect. Neither friend nor foe takes this country for granted now.

People have asked Judge Clark if he thinks Ronald Reagan will run for reelection. He doesn't answer directly, since politics isn't his personal field, but he clearly believes that Ronald Reagan isn't a quitter, that he won't leave the job undone or half done, and that most Americans want to see him finish the job he has begun of rebuilding America.

Greeting Secretary of Defense Caspar Weinberger at the Palace Hotel in New York.

Caspar Weinberger

I VERY MUCH WANTED to interview "Cap" Weinberger but the defense secretary's schedule was too full. I did get to see him and hear him speak at the Palace Hotel in New York to a rather select group known as The President's Committee. Weinberger made a great impression on me. I found him to be, as Selwa Roosevelt said, a dedicated man with humility of style; not at all the arrogant, rigid bureaucrat or the inflexible militaristic hawk his detractors make him out to be.

But the most important thing I learned about Caspar Weinberger is that, in spite of his undeniably strong personality, he always is Ronald Reagan's man. In his all too brief speech to The President's Committee he made this abundantly clear. He said his whole purpose is to follow the president's orders, and those orders are specifically "that the defensive strength of the country must be restored and that the gap in military strength between Soviet Russia and the United States must be filled quickly."

45

There is, of course, much debate over whether or not such a gap exists, but Weinberger made it crystal clear that he and the president have no doubts whatsoever about the gap's existence and that it is formidable. Also, Weinberger made it clear that the growth of this gap must be attributed to two main causes: the slowdown in the growth of productivity in United States industry (particularly the defense industry), and to the actual stealing of our high technology by Soviet agents and their greedy and unscrupulous accomplices.

"The president wants the job of closing the gap done and he wants it done now," Weinberger said. Then he added significantly, "The difference between doing it now and doing it five years from now is a $39 billion saving in defense outlays." (In today's dollars, that is.)

He said that both he and Ronald Reagan recognized that big defense spending is very unpopular, and that closing the military gap with the Russians is a most unpopular task politically speaking.

"However," he added, "the top priority of the Reagan administration is peace and freedom" and he made it plain that there can be no compromise on that.

Then he came to the climactic issue. "The projected cost of our defense buildup for the next six years is $1.6 trillion. That's an enormous figure, but if we build that defense capacity and never have to use it, then the Reagan administration will have been a total success."

I was deeply moved. It was clear to me that Weinberger had just expressed in a single sentence the chief and probably the only real justification for the Reagan/Weinberger defense policy. It seemed to me that every right-thinking American ought to be and probably is willing to pay that cost of assuring that we continue to live under freedom instead of under the yoke of a foreign power or under a dogmatic ideology.

Frankly, very few of us like big defense spending. During most of our history we have maintained very small armed forces, and we tried to disarm after World War II only to have the Russians, the North Koreans, the Chinese Communists and the Viet-Minh compel us to continue to maintain a big military, naval and air establishment.

Since our failure to bring off a military and political victory in Vietnam, there has been a great weariness in the
United States with big defense burdens. Many Americans
no longer see defense questions in clear blacks and whites.

This last attitude leads to a declining faith on the part of
many in a strong defense posture. There are even more
who are skeptical about big defense because of a conviction that no one can win a nuclear conflict. The fiasco of
President Carter's military attempt to rescue the hostages
in Iran and the failure of our military aid to halt the bloody
strife in El Salvador and Guatemala add to this climate of
disillusionment.

Nevertheless, the aggression of the Russians in Afghanistan and their machinations along with those of their Cuban allies in so many parts of Africa and Latin America,
plus the smouldering and unextinguished flames of war in
the Middle East, all compel us to concede the wisdom of
Ronald Reagan's basic defense ideas, even though many
Americans think specific parts of the strategy make no
sense.

At the White House, Robert K. Gubitosi Presidential Staff Assistant telling me all about our First Lady.

Robert Gubitosi

NOT SURPRISINGLY, the feminist movement in this century has caused Americans to pay much more attention to the wives of our presidents, and we have had several first ladies with strong personalities and great capacity for activity and accomplishment.

It began with Eleanor Roosevelt, who was beloved and admired by all except a few jaundiced and puny-minded souls. We have had some admirable first ladies since Mrs. Roosevelt, but I began to suspect soon after Ronald Reagan became president that Nancy Reagan will go down in history as one of the most charming and able women who ever lived in the White House.

Pursuing this idea, I eventually obtained an interview with Robert K. Gubitosi, the presidential staff assistant who is the director of the office of scheduling and advance for the First Lady. That such an office is needed is clear proof of the demands we put nowadays on the time, energies and sympathies of the president's wife.

Bob Gubitosi is a handsome young man who has been on the Reagans' personal staff for four years, the first two while Mr. Reagan was preparing and waging his presidential campaign. He knows both of them well and has come to have a most profound admiration for them as an ideal married couple, and a tremendous respect for Nancy Reagan as both a human being and the finest possible example of a First Lady of the union.

He told me that the Reagans' marriage is an "amazing relationship." "Nancy is devoted to her husband in the most sensitive way," he said, "and the fact that he is the president does not appear to have made the slightest difference in their relationship—he is first of all her husband."

He said that Nancy worries about Ronald a great deal, about his clothes and appearance, his meals and the other things conscientious and sensitive wives worry about on their husbands' behalf, but he doubts seriously if she ever has nagged him even once about anything.

He said he was struck rather early by the fact that after over thirty years of marriage, Nancy and Ronald greet each other after being parted for only a few hours like a pair of newlyweds, with warm hugging and kissing.

"I once said to Nancy, 'You two act as if you were married yesterday.' "

"That's the way he always has made me feel," she answered.

"Sometimes I would see tears in her eyes when she or he would have to go away for only a day or two. You certainly don't expect that in most long-term marriages."

But, Gubitosi told me, she wants what Ronald wants and she doesn't give the fact away if his decisions and desires are not perhaps what she would have chosen. On the contrary, Gubitosi said, "she cranks him up," reinforcing his wants and enthusiasms. Like the president, she wants him to do something fine for America. She feels, as most of us do, that Ronald Reagan paid his dues to become president of the United States by the example he set as governor of California, that he didn't need to seek the presidency for any reason except to put to right the things that had been done wrongly for three and a half decades.

"It is very important," Gubitosi said, "for all of us in the White House to do our best to keep the First Lady happy because she keeps the president happy."

I remarked that it is a shame that the media have not given Mrs. Reagan the tremendous and favorable attention that Eleanor Roosevelt was given. I added that it is also unfortunate that so much attention has been lavished by the print and broadcast reporters on Mrs. Reagan's fondness for as well as good taste in clothes, instead of on her devotion to working to alleviate the consequences of drug addiction and deprivation among the young.

"Well," he replied, "she is becoming more active in things the reporters will take note of. She put on a costume and sang and danced at a Gridiron dinner, and she is appearing on a televison program called 'Diff'rent Strokes,' but what she has done for youthful drug addicts is really astonishing, and it has not gotten the attention it deserves. This work began long before she became the First Lady. I recall that during the presidential campaign we visited a drug rehabilitation center in the New York area called Daytop Village. We had only a limited time but she stayed way beyond the time limit, talking to these kids and hugging them. When we started to leave, some of them hung on her arms. As we started to get into the car, she told me, 'Poor Ronnie! If he gets elected president, I'm going to make him open one of these centers in every city in the land.' "

She hasn't accomplished that, but she's still trying, Gubitosi said.

During the 1980 campaign, Mrs. Reagan and Gubitosi visited a lot of hospitals and had harrowing experiences at some. At one institution she saw a door marked "authorized personnel only," and asked what was behind the door. She was told it was a ward for severely burned children who had been trapped in fires. She asked to be allowed to visit the ward. "The doctors were hesitant but she insisted so they clothed us in sterile gowns and took us in," Gubitosi said. "The children were a fearful sight with large and deep burns and many had lost their hair, but it was a revelation to see the love of this woman, to see her pick these kids up in her arms, and talk to them and caress them and to see the children respond to her."

Gubitosi said Mrs. Reagan had insisted that the reporters tagging along behind her not accompany them into the ward.

"She has reawakened the United States to the fact that the word love still is in the dictionary," Gubitosi told me. "She insists on dealing, both in public and private, with the things most people try hard to avoid dealing with. She not only raises money for such activities, she gets right down to brass tacks and helps the victims personally."

Another example of Mrs. Reagan's loving nature, Gubitosi said, is her concern with the Foster Grandparents program. She wrote a book about this entitled *To Love a Child*, appealing to retired persons to give personal and individual help to disadvantaged children and children with problems. Gubitosi said his own father joined the Foster Grandparents. "He was aging visibly after he retired but he perked up immediately when he became a foster grandfather. It is a wonderful program that helps both the kids and the elderly. Both need to feel wanted and Mrs. Reagan has been surfacing this need to the nation's attention, but not nearly enough has been told about it yet."

Gubitosi said one thing Nancy Reagan will not talk about is whether or not the president will seek reelection. He doubts if she has tried or will try to influence Mr. Reagan or that she could—"Ronald Reagan makes his own decisions."

Gubitosi said the president himself has much the same attitude as Nancy towards children and people who are handicapped. He told of an incident during the New Hampshire primary in 1980. At one rally, a woman in a wheelchair greeted the president warmly and invited him to visit the nursing home where she lived if he came to that rather remote part of the state.

A week later on the tour, Reagan suddenly asked his aides if they weren't rather close to the town where the nursing home was situated. Told that they were, he sent one of his staff to the nursing home to say he would come visit the patient even though a typical New Hampshire spring snowstorm was raging.

When the door at the nursing home was opened to the Reagan man, he was surprised to see all the patients assembled and waiting with a big sign in their midst saying, "Welcome, Governor Reagan."

Perplexed, he asked how they knew the governor was coming since he was just bringing the news. The woman in the wheel chair piped up: "The governor said he would visit us if he got this far north in the state and we knew he'd keep his word."

Gubitosi also reminded me of something many people overlook. At the time we were talking, almost two years had elapsed since the president's inauguration, but he had not really had two full years to push his programs and goals because he was incapacitated to some degree for several months following the assassination attempt by the youthful psychopath Hinckley.

At the State Department with Selwa "Lucky" Roosevelt, Chief of Protocol for President Ronald Reagan.

Selwa Roosevelt

SELWA ROOSEVELT knows a side of Ronald Reagan that is important and special. She is chief of protocol at the state department and formally greets kings, presidents and prime ministers of foreign countries who visit the United States. Her department also looks after the needs of the 6000 or so diplomats assigned to Washington, arranging for diplomatic license plates for their cars, customs courtesies and free entry privileges. She also arranges diplomatic entertainments and oversees seating at formal affairs. She went along on the visit of Queen Elizabeth II and Prince Philip to the west coast of the United States recently to make sure things went off without a hitch.

She is the wife of Archibald Roosevelt, Jr., grandson of President Theodore Roosevelt. She met him while she was a student at Vassar. He now is a director of international relations for the huge Chase Manhattan Bank in New York, but during the early years of their marriage he was in the diplomatic service and held posts in Istanbul, London and Madrid. That's how she learned the intricacies of protocol.

But before getting into Vassar, she was a teenage news-paper reporter in her hometown of Kingsport, Tennessee. Her first job at the age of thirteen was selling perfume in a department store. Her father arrived in the United States at fifteen from Lebanon and ended up in Kingsport, where he had friends and found a job.

Having seen the president meeting with foreign digni-taries and political leaders, Mrs. Roosevelt is impressed by the respect he inspires in these personalities, even those who disagree with the president's ideology and political and economic views.

"These people are enormously impressed by Ronald Reagan's personality, his character and his sincerity," she told me. "They come away thinking, 'There's a man to re-spect, a man who really represents the best in his coun-try.' "

She said she thought this resulted in part from the fact that Mr. Reagan shows great generosity of spirit towards his opponents. "He handles his opponents in the most at-tractive manner and wins their respect, even their affec-tion. For example, he gets along famously with House Speaker Tip O'Neill, who often doesn't agree with him," she said.

She said this personal charm and warmth is most notice-able in his relationship with Mrs. Reagan. "They are the most wonderful couple," she said. "During Queen Eliza-beth's visit with the Reagans in California, when we cele-brated their wedding anniversary on the royal yacht, I re-marked to them, 'You and Mrs. Reagan are a great advertisement for marriage.'

" 'I like that,' the president beamed."

"Everyone notices their obvious affection for the warmth of each other. They hug and kiss and hold hands like newlyweds."

Mrs. Roosevelt hopes the president will run for reelec-tion because he is needed and because he is in such good physical and mental health. "He is one of the most com-fortable men to be with I have ever met because he is al-ways at peace with himself. So, I hope he'll run again and

I'm certain he'll beat the pants off anyone who runs against him."

Saying she is neither an economist nor an expert in political matters, Mrs. Roosevelt nevertheless said she believed firmly that Ronald Reagan's determination to conquer inflation was absolutely essential to the nation's welfare. "That's why most Americans voted for him. The American people are intelligent. They liked all the good things and social progress that years of government spending brought, but they could see the bills piling up and knew they would have to be paid eventually."

She also said it was "unfair" for the press to depict Mr. Reagan as the president of the rich, "because the truth is that it was not the rich who were being squeezed and destroyed by inflation but the middle class and the poor."

She said Ronald Reagan is as concerned as any of the rest of us about unemployment, "but he knows it's a price that has to be paid for ending inflation. Let's ask ourselves what kind of situation we would be in today if Reagan hadn't put a halt to inflation. What would we be up against if the Democratic administration had continued?"

As chief of protocol, she gets a good look at the calibre of people who serve in high places in governments around the world and can compare them with Ronald Reagan and his official family.

"This administration has fine, dedicated people," she said. "The President and Mrs. Reagan, Vice-President and Mrs. Bush, Secretary of State Shultz and Mrs. Shultz and all the others I know are earnest, hard-working persons of great intelligence and integrity."

She concluded that although Americans are proud of their country, they sometimes get discouraged about its state and that the great thing about Ronald Reagan is that, after such a period of discouragement, "he has made it possible for Americans to hold their heads high and be proud again."

Lyn Nofziger, advisor to the president, on his way to New York talking about The President's Committee.

Lyn Nofziger

I OBTAINED some of the most trenchant observations about Ronald Reagan from Lyn Nofziger, who was a political adviser to the president during his first year in the White House.

Nofziger told me he quit the job simply because he doesn't like working for the government for long. He said persons who stay in government service for long periods acquire illusions. "They begin to love the feeling of power and to think they have a right to it and to imagine they are indispensable or at least essential; they become part of our biggest national problem," he explained.

So he quit and went into business as a public relations man and political fund raiser.

Nofziger first became captivated by Ronald Reagan as a youngish reporter for the Copley newspaper chain in California. He told an older colleague, "This man could be president some day."

" 'Don't be naïve,' my friend told me, 'he'll be in enough

trouble if he's elected governor. He's only an actor reading lines, not a man of political substance.' "

But Nofziger was more and more impressed as time passed and rather against his will, as he recalls matters, he was gradually drawn into the Reagan campaign organization. He worked in the gubernatorial races and in both the 1976 and 1980 presidential campaigns and found that his early intimations about Reagan had blossomed into hero worship.

He told me he thinks it's terribly important that Mr. Reagan be reelected, "and I'm confident he will run again. I don't see how he can not run again if his health remains good. He's not going to walk away from a job that's not finished."

But Nofziger said the president ought to let us know now that he is thinking seriously about running again. "The time for that has come and all the people in office need to get a clear indication from the White House of his inclination and intentions."

Nofziger surprised me a little by not putting his finger directly on ending inflation as Mr. Reagan's greatest accomplishment to date. He said rather that the great accomplishment was changing the national debate from "how much we must spend" to "how much we must cut spending." Of course that bears on inflation, but there's a subtle and vital difference in emphasis. It is a recognition that inflation and the ills of American society cannot be cured by mere bookkeeping and financial juggling; that, admirable as the efforts of Federal Reserve Chief Paul Volcker have been, they could not have worked by themselves without the Reagan insistence on cost cutting and personal sacrifice by many citizens."

"We no longer debate about how to expand government," Nofziger said, "but about how we should reduce governmental activity." But at the same time, Nofziger praised Mr. Reagan for refusing to knuckle under to those who raise alarms about the economy and object to a sensible improvement in national defense.

Nofziger is one who believes, as I do, that the unemployment picture is being blown up and exaggerated by not

taking into account the existence and growth of the underground economy and by the statistical methods we use in
counting the jobless. He told me that the reason the politicians and the press do not come sufficiently to grips with
the menace of the underground economy is that the issue
is too new and there is too little hard, reliable information
about it. Also, he said, dealing with the underground economy necessarily will involve shaking up and reshaping our
entire tax structure. "That's a huge undertaking and everybody shrinks at the prospect of tackling it," he said, "but
the underground economy is growing and becoming such a
cancer that we will have to deal with it. A struggle over it
will come."

He said he is sure Nancy Reagan will not object to
Ronald's running for reelection and that she accepts the
fact that he has not changed basically in his seventeen
years in politics. And that, he said, may be the most important thing about Reagan—"He himself has not changed
but he has changed the direction of the country."

"It's an historical maxim that all power corrupts but
Ronald Reagan is the shining exception. Power hasn't and
can't corrupt him. He is an honest, forthright and honor-
able man, a Godfearing man. He never has forgotten his
humble beginnings. He is justly proud of his success but
he never has been tempted to change his principles or his
approach to life. He never has become arrogant or pom-
pous; you can kid him and joke with him," Nofziger added.

This makes Ronald Reagan the ideal political candidate,
he said. "He invariably rises to the occasion. Moreover,
people soon learn it doesn't pay to make Reagan angry: he
will hit back hard. Also, he doesn't have any of the serious
flaws or frailties that have marred the personalities and
spoiled the careers of many otherwise able and brilliant
politicians. You don't have to worry about Ronald Reagan
getting drunk or going chasing after women, for example,"
he added with a grin.

The fact that Reagan has a great sense of humor and is a
talented raconteur also endears him to political mentors
and shepherds.

PART TWO

America's Greatest
Hour of Trial

I

Reagan's Triumph

RONALD REAGAN'S SECOND YEAR in the White House saw inflation as measured by the consumer price index fall for several months in a row to an annual rate of 1.5 percent.

In February, 1983, the consumer price index actually dropped for only the second time since 1965; the drop was 0.2%.

That has to be one of the greatest victories ever achieved by an American president. For the ex-Hollywood cowboy actor, it was a personal triumph that could in time rank with George Washington's feat in putting the infant nation's finances and economy in order virtually overnight.

Most monetary and fiscal experts regard 1.5 percent as the limit for an acceptable level of inflation in a year. If the United States can hold inflation at this level for a prolonged period we will be the only major power with a free enterprise economy in the western world to do so. Only some of the East Asian nations have managed to come anywhere near this, and they have done so only at the cost of great austerity and few government services for the masses.

An absolutely stable economy with no inflation at all may appear to be ideal, but history indicates that a very mild inflation usually has been a nation's only way, or at

61

least the most desirable way, of paying for social progress.*
Those periods of history in the western world during the
past thousand years during which there was absolutely no
inflation or a pronounced deflation, have rather uniformly
been periods of great stagnation, frustration and suffering,
often with widespread starvation.

But in the third and final quarters of this century we
have experienced a simultaneous serious inflation and
stagnation that is unprecedented, at least among English-
speaking peoples. Starting with the decision of President
Lyndon Johnson to prosecute the war in Vietnam without
putting the country on a wartime economic footing, and
continuing through the many tides of confusion in the Nixon, Ford and Carter administrations, the great American
economy has been increasingly afflicted by this "stagflation," which for several protracted periods pushed monetary inflation up to annual rates approaching 15 percent with
the interest rate for prime business loans rising as high as
20½ percent on occasion.

To be sure, even these unprecedented inflation levels in
the United States are nothing to compare with inflation of
40 to well over 100 percent a year experienced by Japan,
Brazil, Argentina, Israel, Italy and many other great nations since World War II. Other countries also have experienced runaway interest rates, but now in the 1980s it is
American interest rates that are plaguing our economy and
that of the entire free enterprise world.

In appraising the progress of the Reagan Administration's struggle to overcome inflation and high interest
rates, and deciding whether "Reaganomics" is the monstrous evil so many persons presently contend it is, we
must first recognize that the Reagan crusade is a war, and
you cannot fight a war without casualties. We have to
accept this fact if we are going to win the war against
stagflation.

During a shooting war and after peace has been declared, we nowadays compensate the casualties or their
survivors by disability payments, death benefits, educa-

*Will Inflation Destroy America, by Arthur Milton, Citadel Press, New
York, 1977.

tional opportunities and other kinds of financial relief. This was not always so. Throughout most of history people's lives and liberties were at the disposal of their rulers and feudal masters, who were in no way obliged to compensate them or their survivors if they died in war. Their lives were the outright property of their lords.

That has been changed, but there still is no feasible way to compensate the casualties of economic warfare or their survivors because any financial relief given them simply has the Malthusian effect of destroying or delaying economic recovery. In the ancient world and right down to the middle of this century, in many parts of the world the casualties of all kinds of economic distress—famines, Great Depressions, and runaway inflation—simply were allowed to starve *en masse,* and when enough of the victims had starved to death to create a great scarcity of productive workers, demand for labor rose and economic recovery set in.

Modern American society will not tolerate such a brutal solution. Communist society does tolerate it: millions starved or died of diseases brought on by deprivation and malnutrition in Russia in order to put Marxist-Leninist ideas in power, and millions died in eastern Europe after World War II as the price of imposing Stalinist power and theory.

Although we will not knowingly allow people to starve in the United States, neither can we expect or hope to bring about recovery without extensive deprivation and frustration. Some families are experiencing economic disasters that are irreversible and irreparable. It is a repetition of what happened after the 1929 stock market crash which brought on a depression that lasted a dozen years. The struggle then was not against inflation but against deflation and stagnation amid apparent surpluses of practically everything people consumed or used. Millions of words have been written about the causes of the 1930s depression and there still is no general agreement as to what caused the collapse, but there is agreement that illusions and clinging to outmoded ideas contributed much to bringing on the disaster.

If we will reflect a moment on that terrible economic

defeat of 1929, we will realize that, statistically at least, our troubles are not nearly so great now as those our forebears faced then. The defaults and bankruptcies of that era dwarfed anything we are experiencing now. Unemployment reached an official level of 16 percent but is believed by some historians to have been much nearer 25 percent because many of the jobless were not registered and there was little public experience in 1929 in gathering employment statistics. Wages were slashed by 10 to 30 percent in two years and we had no unemployment insurance and no Social Security system to cushion the deadening blows of the depression hammer. The jobless in the 1930s simply were dependent on relatives or religious and public charities.

World War II took us out of the great depression finally, but we had made substantial progress toward working our way out of it by 1940.

The situation we are in today also is not nearly so bad as the peoples of the eleven defeated Confederate states faced in 1865. For most of the population of the South, both white and black, economic stagnation then endured for seventy years, until about 1935. But today the South and the Sunbelt are the strongest and fastest-growing regions in the country.

Our recovery from these two great setbacks should reassure us that there is no reason to feel that, now that we have broken the back of inflation, we cannot solve the terrible problems created by interest rates and the loss of much of our technological edge and productivity lead. But just as it took a dozen years to recover from the Great Depression, the struggle to overcome our present problems will not be short or easy. As President Reagan has said a number of times, it would be extremely naïve to think that in one four-year presidential term we can completely undo the consequences of thirty-five years of post-war extravagance, irresponsibility, sloppiness and the delusion that we had become too big and strong to have to worry about the winds of economic and social change in the world.

The recovery this time could be less fearsome for individuals because we do have the mechanisms of a welfare state and because the common people now have political power and know how to use it. This was not the case in 1929. But as a nation we are in a far more precarious position than we were in the early 1930s, and unless we recognize how precarious our nation's position is and unite to solve it, the ultimate impact on all of us as individuals could be dire.

The statement that we will not tolerate starvation or total deprivation and frustration for the victims of the war against stagflation should not blind us to the grim fact that there still are plenty of people in the world who not only would tolerate such a grim destructive solution of the dilemmas of our times, but would welcome it. We have seen millions perish in China, Vietnam, Cambodia, parts of the Middle East and Africa and many thousands die in Latin-America in political strife motivated by hunger and frustration.

Violence growing out of socio-economic conflict is the most significant characteristic of our era. And it is precisely those persons who are most vociferous in their clamor against Reaganomics who are most likely to cause violence to break out on a large scale in the United States. The do-gooders of this world are the lovers of violence, the fanatics who believe their ends and aims justify mass murder, who swallow whole ideologies that preach, at first in secret, then openly, that all who oppose them must be liquidated in time and that it is perfectly justifiable to kill millions of people just to get rid of them. It would be too much to accuse all leftists of being homicidal hypocrites but it is a matter of record that both Adolf Hitler and Benito Mussolini began their political careers as Socialists.

So we cannot blind ourselves to the possible or probable consequences if we eventually lose the struggle against stagflation. A bloodbath is the logical thing to expect.

The precariousness of our situation grows out of a long list of circumstances, including these:

—A staggering and frightening burden of military outlays.
—Cumulative inflation amounting to 300 to 500 percent over the past twenty-five years in various sectors of our economy.

—The accumulation of a crushing national debt resulting from many successive years of federal deficits.

—The depletion of our natural resources as the result of three large wars and a huge burden of military and other aid to allies around the world, many of them of extremely dubious reliability.

—An energy shortage that, while it has eased momentarily, could return overnight to threaten us with economic ruin.

—A huge annual foreign trade deficit growing out of the inability of many of our major industries to compete successfully on world markets. They can't compete at home either, so our imports are excessive.

—A steady loss of our technological edge in industry after industry.

—A baffling productivity decline in many industries.

—A failure of American management philosophy, which was so successful two decades ago, to achieve either growth or profitability in the 1980s.

—A steady drift of many American industries into offshore manufacturing—i.e. "the export of jobs."

—Almost total inability of big business, big union labor and government to cooperate in the national interest.

—The development of a lawless, untaxed underground economy that threatens to become more than half as big as the legal economy.

—The near collapse of the construction industry, particularly in home building, so that the American working-class family no longer can afford either to own or rent living space.

—The steady erosion and near destruction of small business.

—The near collapse of such basic industries as steel, automobiles, aluminum, aircraft, lumber, cement, other building materials and petrochemicals.

—The low profitability of American agriculture in spite of enjoying enormous domestic and foreign markets and an amazing level of mechanization and automation.

—Inability to make our coal industry with its abundant mine reserves profitable.

—The shift of capital and human energies from useful production to speculative non-productive enterprises such as casino gambling, professional and big-time college sports, extravagant theatrical entertainment, videogames and a wide range of financial and promotional operations that create nothing useful—only speculative gains and wasteful conspicuous consumption.

—An enormous growth of crime that has increased the cost of doing business for practically every merchant, every professional and every corporation and institution.

—A large diversion of capital into crime, especially into the narcotics traffic.

—A staggering diversion of capital from useful production into mergers that make quick profits for stock speculators, lawyers and management insiders, but usually result only in reduced competition, lower efficiency and reduced production, creating scarcities in the economy.

—A diversion of capital from the normal securities markets that has caused a serious undervaluation in the market of corporate stocks and bonds even in relation to industry's diminished profitability. This hurts the economy as a whole. People cannot raise enough money by selling securities unless they are willing to take enormous losses from what they originally paid for the securities, so they are forced to borrow for their needs at the current ruinous interest rates. This forces interest rates higher still.

—A short-sighted preoccupation of business with short-term profits, which often are not realized, at the expense of long-term growth and technological superiority.

—The degradation of products and the shift of much of industry to an economy of shoddy scarcity instead of one of plenty and quality.

—Unrealistic, high-financial expectations of the average American family, leading to an extravagant and wasteful standard of living and personal financial irresponsibility.

More critical in the long run than any of these specific problems is the overall human problem. The late prime minister of Israel, David Ben-Gurion, once said that the Israelis' remarkable economic and technological achievements in their arid country were simply a matter of calculating the needed amounts of water and minerals to add to the soil and applying them. What had been critical and dif-

ficult, Ben-Gurion said, was the problem of how to moti-
vate people to come to Israel and stay, to endure the danger and hard work that made the Israeli miracle possible.

So today in America our biggest problem actually is to
restore the optimism, altruism, ingenuity and perse-
verence that enabled us to achieve such greatness in the
world in the nineteenth century and the first sixty years of
this century.

The ultimate and often the immediate causes of all these
sombre specific problems vary. For example, the credit
card, high-pressure broadcast consumer advertising and
easy airline travel that lure people to buy a vast variety of
luxury goods and services, all have contributed to consumer extravagance and irresponsibility and a selfish attitude towards life.

Inflation and high interest rates are two readily discernible causes that are common to almost every one of the
twenty-five specific critical problems I have just listed.
But of course, these specific problems are contributors to
inflation and high interest rates to an even greater degree
than they are caused by them.

So we have the old phenomenon of the vicious circle:
cause becomes effect and effect becomes cause and neither seems curable.

The summer of 1982 brought additional evidence that
inflation indeed was subsiding. The labor department reported that the persistent upward wage spiral was being
broken. Wage and fringe benefit boosts still were rising
faster than the consumer price index but not nearly as fast
as in 1980 and 1981. They appeared to be dropping below
6 percent in the second quarter, compared with 10 percent
for all of 1981. Various surveys by management consulting
firms predicted a further slowdown of the spiral in the second half of the year, and the *Wall Street Journal* said the
unions were accepting the slowdown with remarkably little protest.

Another indication that the Reagan policies are working
is that inflation as measured by the prices of industrial machinery and equipment, and by the cost of construction,
was about halved in the first six months of 1982.

A survey made by the Kemper Insurance Group showed that price increases of industrial machinery and equipment were only 2.27 percent in the first half of 1982, as against 5.36 percent in the first half of 1981, while construction costs climbed only 2.21 percent in the first six months of 1982, against 4.75 percent a year earlier.

But the biggest indication of the Reagan success may well prove to be the continuing strength of the U.S. dollar in the foreign exchange markets. France, Mexico and Argentina have had to devalue their currencies against the dollar, and the British pound, the Canadian dollar and many other currencies have fallen against the dollar. The dollar price of gold has gone down even more dramatically.

This is hurting American exports somewhat but it reflects a concensus of foreign opinion that the U.S. economy is gaining in stability and makes it a little easier to pay for our big imports.

Now that President Reagan has taken the first step with his austerity program, it is up to the rest of us to take matters in our own hands and go the rest of the way. We must compel the Congress to find workable solutions and adopt them no matter how unpalatable they are politically. And the attack must be on a wide front. Every one of the twenty-five critical problems just cited must be attacked simultaneously.

President Reagan undoubtedly believed, when he first took office, that conquering inflation would be less difficult than it has proved. It is a practical certainty that he was surprised when his program of simultaneous austerity and tax cuts resulted in rising interest rates and did not create jobs rather soon. He also was surprised by the harsh recession and the brutal slash in corporate profits. The overriding reason for the surprising turn of events almost certainly is the cumbersomeness of our huge government machinery and the incompetence and lack of dedication of so many of our bureaucrats and elected officials. Our government, it appears, cannot or will not act promptly or with adequate vigour except in wartime.

Nevertheless, it would be naïve and criminally deceptive to think that government and the politicians are solely to blame for the mess we are in. We all are to blame, including business, particularly big business, and the savants of the university graduate business schools.

How and why was inflation reduced in the first half of 1982? Did Ronald Reagan accomplish it? Was it the result of delayed reaction to the policies of Jimmy Carter's administration, or just the natural consequence of severe recession? Perhaps the recession was inevitable and would have occurred without the Reagan austerity budgets, but could a recession actually have slowed inflation without the budget cuts? It seems highly doubtful.

It is more logical to conclude that, in spite of the roller coaster ride the national economy took during Mr. Reagan's first year in the White House, it ultimately was the austerity program that curbed inflation. It was the perseverance and political savvy the president displayed in getting his major program planks through Congress and the backbone he showed in dealing with such critical matters as the air traffic controllers' strike—in short, his willingness to pay the price in casualties that brought the victory.

In any case, inflation was only diminished. The 1.5 percent annual level to which it was reduced for several months in succession does not mean that all prices are now up only that much from a year ago. In the first place there was sharp rise in inflation in May and prices of many things still are going up at clips of 5 to 15 percent a year. Unions are still trying to get wage and fringe boosts of 15 to 30 percent a year. Agents for players in the National Football League talk of starting salaries for high draft rookies of $150,000 a year plus bonuses of $250,000 to $500,000 for signing. There aren't enough professional football players to have an overall impact on inflation but this is a revealing symptom of the prevailing national psychology. Too many of us are living in "an era of wonderful nonsense," such as the late 1920s were—"Get it right now. To hell with tomorrow and to hell with everybody else in the country so long as I get rich in a hurry."

A great many persons are bound to believe high interest rates are the price Mr. Reagan paid for his victory over inflation and that they will be with us for a long time. That leads logically to the conclusion that there are only two ways to bring interest rates down:

—Expand the money supply rapidly. That should make it possible for the banks to lend at much lower rates. But it certainly would lead to rapidly rising prices and renewed inflation.
—Greatly expand the output of goods and services without expanding the money supply by forcing available capital out of speculative, luxury and service industries into production of goods that are highly salable on both domestic and foreign markets.

The first course would compel us to live under an indexed economy with a soft currency worthless in international trade, and with ever-mounting government deficits and rigorous government controls on imports and most domestic business activity, including wages. Tax evasion would mushroom as would the growth of the underground economy. The spread of crime would accelerate and the values of American society would deteriorate and disintegrate. Our remaining power and prestige in the world would disappear rather fast.

The painful process of increasing productivity by belt tightening is much more attractive. That alone is feasible.

By the sheer weight of his character and without taking any active steps, President Reagan achieved another triumph at the start of his administration that had eluded and frustrated Jimmy Carter for more than a year.

The Iranian regime of the Ayatollah Khomeini released the fifty-odd American hostages who had been held for so long at the embassy in Tehran.

There have been some revelations from Iranian and other sources in the past two years about this infamous incident. Very recent Iranian revelations indicate that the Ayatollah's fanatical followers were motivated less by their professed anti-Americanism and the goal of getting Shah Mohammed Reza Pahlevi returned to Iran to stand trial than by a determination to justify the destruction of the remnants of the interim Bahktiar government that succeeded the Shah, and to consolidate the power of the reactionary mullahs and create a modern revival of a medieval theocracy.

Be that as it may, nothing the Carter administration or the United Nations did on behalf of the hostages budged the Khomeini extremists and there is no reason to believe they would have released the hostages any time soon if Carter had been reelected, but Ronald Reagan's mere accession to the White House freed them. The Iranians put on a big show of recalcitrance and dragged out the actual release for several days but didn't succeed in fooling the world. They did not get any ransom for the hostages, only the unfreezing of Iranian assets in the United States that had been seized.

The failure of Jimmy Carter's ill-planned helicopter mission to rescue the hostages had convinced Khomeini that Carter was indecisive and helpless and that he could hold the hostages indefinitely. But it was apparent at the time and is much clearer today that the Ayatollah had sized up Ronald Reagan correctly and realized that retaining the hostages after he was sworn in as president was too great a risk to be contemplated. He and his associates saw Ronald Reagan as a man of tremendous character and determination.

Thus, the freeing of the hostages was new proof of the overwhelming importance of character and personality in high office and public affairs. Reagan's character succeeded where diplomacy and half-hearted military activity had failed.

II

The Enemy Is Us

In the July-August, 1980, edition of the *Harvard Business Review* there appeared an article entitled *Managing Our Way to Economic Decline* which eventually shook much of the management world rather like a tornado.

It was written by two young Harvard business professors, Robert J. Hayes and William J. Abernathy, and it was followed by a stream of articles and speeches all in the same vein, which an interview in *The New York Times* (May 30, 1982) summed up as "We have found the enemy and it is us."

Actually a lot of other well-informed persons both in the United States and abroad have been saying some of the same things as Hayes and Abernathy, but when the message that American management has been deliberately led astray by the teachings of university business schools comes from Harvard, the oldest and most prestigious management school in the world, it is almost earthshaking.

The views of Hayes and Abernathy go a long way towards explaining why American corporate management, which was so overshadowingly successful and put the United States in such a dominant position in the world's economy in the 1950s and 1960s, has petered out and failed so miserably in the 1970s and early 1980s. Very bluntly, Hayes and Abernathy have been telling American

73

businessmen that although excessive and heavy-handed government regulation, powerful and sometimes avaricious labor unions, the energy crisis, the devilish cleverness of the Japanese and the decline of the work ethic in America all hurt, they are not the main causes of the disaster.

The real cause, they say, is the MBA executive's philosophy and his ivory tower approach to management. They charge, for example, that the average MBA executive never gets any closer to the factories he is running than looking at the reports and pictures in his briefcase, and that this absentee management, which is much worse than absentee ownership, is the main reason so many bedrock American industries are withering in the harsh winds of foreign competition. To put it another way, all American management now has drifted away from basic common sense. As a result, Hayes and Abernathy contend, American industry is being starved and run in a short-sighted, sloppy, uninspired fashion by managers who have no interest in the business the company is engaged in or its products. They are concerned only with the figures their computers spew out, and have an exaggerated, totally unrealistic conception of the importance of short-term profit, which is all they really believe in. As I have often said, theory without practice is impractical.

The interview in *The New York Times* said that Hayes and Abernathy thought the average business school graduate believes all business can be run like an investment portfolio; you don't try to cure a sick stock, you dump it. So the MBA isn't much concerned with helping businesses by sound management—just dump the ailing dogs and buy something better. Suppose our hospitals and schools were run that way—don't bother to try to cure the seriously ill patients, let 'em die quickly and get some more promising patients in their beds. Don't try to help the slow learners at school, kick the dumb clucks out and recruit somebody else. Too many executives run their business with fear and constant intimidation. As a result, we run out of useful human material too soon.

Such an attitude is just as wasteful in business as it

would be in medicine and education. It wastes people, business assets and facilities and economic opportunities.

Hayes and Abernathy contend that this ivory-tower, bottom-line, short-term-profit philosophy breeds other absurd evils. For example, it exalts "managerial remote control," management by computer printouts with a total lack of familiarity or concern about actual line operations such as production, design, marketing and selling or of personnel motivation and other people problems.

Much worse, they confirm something many others have complained about in the attitudes of young MBAs. They are too much in a hurry. This attitude was described in *The New York Times* interview as "a seductive doctrine that promises the bright students a quick path to the top and that piles its rewards on executives who force impressive short-term performance at indeterminate cost to long-term health. Fearing any dip in today's profits, American companies keep research and technology on short rations, skipping investment in facilities critically needed to insure competiveness tomorrow."

I might add that this shortsightedness shows that the MBAs who are guilty of it don't know any more about sound investment philosophy than they do about management, so it is stupid for them to say they can run corporations like an investment portfolio. I have been in the money business for almost four decades and one of the first things I learned about it and believe now more than ever is that "the patient investor gets compounded while the impatient investor gets confounded." I suspect it's much the same with patient and impatient managers.

The midsummer 1980 article drew more attention than any piece ever published by the *Harvard Business Review*, according to one of the editors. However, even though it shook the management establishment, it hasn't had much practical effect as yet. Abernathy created a later stir by succeeding in quantifying the consequences of American management mistakes and other factors that give Japanese automobile manufacturers such an advantage in the U.S. market. He put the Japanese advantage at fifteen hundred dollars per car.

Of course some top corporate managers are taking Hayes and Abernathy and others who have said some of the same things to heart. General Electric, Ford Motor Company, General Motors and TRW, Incorporated, all have praised Hayes and Abernathy for their rebellion against the prevailing establishment management philosophy and announced their intention to profit by it.

In their succeeding articles and speeches, Hayes and Abernathy have attacked more specific evils of current management attitudes. They have condemned the currently popular management concept of "discounted cash flow" as a way of killing the goose that lays the golden eggs and as a convenient way for a manager to duck making hard decisions. The theory of "discounted cash flow" is that a buck in hand today is worth more than several bucks hanging on the bush to be picked later, precisely the old "bird in the hand is worth two in the bush" proverb. Now, that is perfectly valid for many situations, but Hayes and Abernathy say that when you try to apply it to everything it becomes absurd. It becomes an easy excuse for not making necessary or desirable capital investments, for example, and it enables managers to rationalize cowardly decisions by deciding the long-term profit prospect isn't good enough to justify the investment. In fact, a manager can't possibly know enough about the future to be sure of that.

Let's take an example. It is suggested that the company spend $75,000 on a certain machine or process improvement. Sitting down at his computer terminal, the executive in charge figures that under the discounted cash flow theory the $75,000 investment must return $350,000 in profit in five years. Considering inflation and other hazards, he gets cold feet and decides not to make the investment even though the computer tells him rather clearly that the company may be forced out of this particular line of business within three years if he doesn't spend the $75,000. But, he figures, what the hell, if I show a good profit this year, I'll find another job next year, so why risk that $75,000 now? Never mind the company's long-range problem.

A lot of disheartening experiences over several years finally decided Hayes and Abernathy to write the controver-

sial article. Abernathy told *The New York Times* that because the article was so emotional and was not backed up
by references in the usual precise academic manner, they
were apprehensive about the reception it would get. But
about the time it appeared, Hayes and Abernathy began to
see bits and pieces of similar rebellious ideas appearing in
other management periodicals and in the speeches of some
business leaders, so the reaction to their article was not
chilly or explosive, but highly favorable on the whole.

Among the experiences that led to the article was a visit
to a senior management seminar conducted by Harvard at
Vevery, Switzerland. Hayes was astonished to discover
that only two of the senior executives attending were the
least bit interested in operational management. This was
no surprise to me. In countless hundreds of conventions I
have attended over the years, rarely did I find executives
interested in anything other than their own aggrandize-
ment. What a pity most are so small not to realize it is people who count.

The Vevery seminar was a humiliating experience for
Abernathy, he told *The New York Times*. He had worked in
Germany during the high tide of American managerial
dominance, and now he felt like a poor relation to managers from other countries. He was angry because American industrial might and managerial prestige had fallen so
low that "I felt poor in Switzerland."

Then there was the time Hayes was teaching a class of
European businessmen. When he began reciting the conventional excuses for the decline of American industrial
power—strong labor unions, government interference and
an earlier baby boom and a subsequent tapering off of population growth—the Europeans laughed in his face. They
said they all had the same problems but that their productivity and profitability were improving, so why was American business lagging so? Hayes said he was confused and
shaken by this experience.

Frequent visits to the plants of Japanese automakers and
to Detroit also contributed to Hayes's and Abernathy's ultimate rebellion.

It has been asserted widely for several years that the Japanese automakers' advantage resulted from low labor costs, vigorous government support and a homogeneous culture that made all Japanese cooperate in order to compete successfully. Hayes and Abernathy do not think these are the key factors. They think the real answer is good management in Japan and poor management in Detroit. The big thing about Japanese automobile management, they say, is that it pays constant attention to basics, technological innovation, cleaner, more attractive factories, more preventive machinery maintenance and strict quality control.

On the other hand, they found practically everything in Detroit sloppy. There seemed to be a preoccupation with avoiding big changes and with making small cost cuts that were self-defeating in the long run. This can lead to far too much rigidity. The cost cuts, small as they are, are achieved only by avoiding innovation and sacrificing technological competitiveness.

And although Hayes and Abernathy did not say so, motorists know that none of these small cost savings were passed on to them. They all were absorbed into profit, overhead or wages. At least this was the case until the recent rash of price rebates was instituted by the American automakers.

Hayes and Abernathy feel that efficiency and technological superiority are much more likely to be the result of turbulence in management and design rather than of a love of order and standardization. They feel that cosmetic design changes like fins and other styling gimmicks have nothing to do with real technology. And they insist that marketing gimmicks and even very broad distribution are no substitute for real technological superiority in automobiles and other sophisticated manufactures.

I have seen similar shortsightedness in the life insurance industry, with which I have long been connected: Here is where the executive, not generally having the benefit of knowing what the consumer needs, wants or can afford, lets the business deteriorate for lack of attention to basics. I call this heads-in-the-sand management.*

*See *How Your Life Insurance Policies Rob You,* by Arthur Milton, Citadel Press, New York, 1981.

It was easy for the United States to maintain technological superiority in the 1950s, simply because the rest of the world still was recovering from World War II. It has been more difficult in the 1970s and now, but Hayes and Abernathy feel the difficulty is mostly of our own making.

However, leaders of many large industries don't think so, or at least will not admit it. Recently the aircraft, automotive, steel, cement, petrochemical and many other industries have been complaining bitterly to Washington that they no longer can compete either in the home market or abroad against foreign industry because foreign industries and foreign governments don't live by the same economic and trade rules and philosophy that we do. These industries complain that Japan, France, Britain, Germany, Italy and the Scandinavian and Latin-American countries and some of the east Asian countries discriminate against American products of all kinds while subsidizing their own products at home and on world markets in myriad ways in order to provide jobs for their people.

The big complaint is that industry in these countries does not operate on a for-profit basis as we understand profit, and not having to show an early profit according to our yardstick, they have a big competitive advantage. As a result, the French have taken over our dominant position in the world market for small and middle-size helicopters; the European Airbus Industrie consortium has grabbed off a huge share of the heavy aircraft market long dominated by Boeing, McDonnell Douglas and Lockheed. Other industries report the same problems.

What it boils down to is that our mixed economy compounded of Adam Smith's laissez-faire ideas and Keynes's theories of government intervention seems to have its priorities wrong, which is exactly what Hayes and Abernathy contend.

What they say has been said many times before, and was ignored because some of those who said it were rather crackpotty on other matters. William Jennings Bryan said it in his famous Cross of Gold speech. The great American economist, Thorstein Veblen, said it in his last book in 1921, and Howard Scott, the founder of the technocratic movement, said it in the early 1930s. They all said you can't assign top priority to profit and maintain a viable national economy for long. Veblen and Scott both said top priority has to be given to technology and the future, not profit alone. Now Harvard's Hayes and Abernathy are telling us the same thing.

Will we listen this time?

Two very recent books have shed further extremely interesting light on the conclusions of Hayes and Abernathy about excessive concern for short-term, bottom-line profit.

Two management consultants of the prestigious McKinsey & Company, Thomas J. Peters and Robert H. Waterman, Jr., spent three years researching and writing *In Search of Excellence* (Harper & Row, New York, 1982), a study of the management philosophies and practices of forty blue-chip American corporations which they regarded as the best run in the country. Their aim was to show that the management of these companies is as good or better than the best Japanese management.

Significantly, they concluded that none of these companies go by what is taught at Harvard, Stanford and the other big-time university graduate business schools. Instead, Peters and Waterman wrote, these best run of American companies put their faith in getting good people and motivating them to work hard, not in systems. Peters and Waterman worked out a list of eight common concerns these companies displayed. The list was topped by "a bias for action," staying in there pitching all the time, and maintaining an entrepreneurial attitude by keeping operating units as small as practicable.

But the most noticeable thing about this list of desirable traits was that concern for the bottom line wasn't even mentioned! Apparently, these very successful companies believe management is an evolutionary affair—if you do the necessary things right, you naturally will get to the bottom line in pretty good shape.

The other book is *The Deindustrialization of America* (Basic Books, New York, 1979), by Barry Bluestone and Bennett Harrison. Bluestone teaches at Boston College, Harrison at MIT. They say the book was commissioned in 1979 as a research project by a coalition of trade unions and community organizations up in arms over factory closings and the movement of production abroad by American corporations. They argue that from 30 million to 50 million jobs were lost as a result of these plant closings and they call this phenomenon "the deindustrialization" of the country.

Their prime thesis is that greedy, shortsighted concern with bottom-line profit without regard to the interests of the American public on the part of corporate management and shareholder interests motivated this deindustrialization and has caused great suffering and a great reduction in the nation's strength.

Their book has been criticized rather roundly as being an exaggerated and biased ideological tract rather than a work based on objective research. The critics accused Bluestone and Harrison of simplistic sensationalism, an unduly pessimistic tone and of ignoring such countervailing facts as that total employment in the United States rose from 78 million to 99 million during the very period in which they complain so many jobs were lost.

Nevertheless, these same critics said Bluestone and Harrison were right in pointing out that the American system does not sufficiently take into account the harsh cost of change to its victims, those who are displaced from their jobs or uprooted from their places in society. But the critics could not agree that the so-called deindustrialization had resulted in maximizing corporate profits, as Bluestone and Harrison claimed. On the contrary, profits seemed to have gone down on the whole. But they conceded that some managements may have been motivated by short-sighted, near-term, bottom-line profit concerns in moving factory production abroad.

More and more thoughtful people are turning thumbs down on excessive concern for the short-term bottom line.

III

The Glories of the Past

PRESIDENT REAGAN clearly is determined to make a dramatic start toward restoring the United States to the position of overshadowing economic power we enjoyed in the 1950s and 1960s.

This vast power really began in the 1890s, although Europe and the rest of the world did not actually realize how majestic our economic stature had become until World War I. But from about 1916 on there was no doubt in the mind of any well-informed person anywhere on earth that the United States could muster more economic resources and strength than Europe, Asia, Africa and Latin America put together. Even during the darkest days of the Great Depression of the 1930s when we wrestled with severe problems of stagnation, we were better off by far than any other nation in the world, and our power continued to grow until the 1970s, even though, as Winston Churchill once observed, we had squandered our natural resources freely in order to save the world from fascist slavery.

In order to better understand what we have lost in the past decade we should take a swift look backward at the whole story of the development of the economy of our country from earliest colonial times.

Adam Smith's great book *The Wealth of Nations* and our *Declaration of Independence* both appeared in 1776. It is doubtful if more than one or two of the American leaders who assembled in Philadelphia to declare the colonies free from the rule of George III had even heard of Smith, and certainly they had not read his book; but *The Wealth of Nations* and *The Declaration of Independence* attacked the same economic order, mercantilism.

Except for a few brief experiments with free trade, mercantilism had been the prevailing western economic system for two hundred and fifty years. It had succeeded feudalism, and under feudalism land was the sole source and measure of wealth. Anyone who did not own productive land was a slave, a vagabond or, at the very least, a social and political cipher no matter how talented. The greatest landowner was the church. As the feudal barons and the church became less powerful and the kings became absolute monarchs, a mercantilist middle class developed and a mercantile system of politics and economics gained sway. Under mercantilism, gold and money were the main measures of wealth, although land still was important. Labor remained oppressed and shackled under mercantilism and enjoyed even fewer privileges than under feudalism.

Mercantilism can be defined as a system of government intervention to promote national prosperity and the power of the king or, as in the case of Venice, of the republic. But national prosperity under mercantilism did not include prosperity for the common people, only for the Crown and the aristocracy or the mercantile oligarchy. Some historians maintain that mercantilism always was far more concerned with political power and privilege than with economics. But the economic essence of mercantilism was the accumulation of gold by constantly expanded export trade and the use of high customs duties, quotas, embargos and outright monopolies enforced by military and naval power to limit imports.

The costs of manufactured goods to be exported were kept low by extreme repression of the farmers and other workers. As under feudalism, the peasants and artisans were kept immobilized for the most part, kept in ignorance and were deprived of any political rights and of most civil rights. Naked military force was used to impose a rigorously stratified society and extremely low wages so the aristocracy and the mercantile class could live in luxury and accumulate enormous fortunes.

Between them, Adam Smith's great book and *The Declaration of Independence* eventually destroyed mercantilism in the English-speaking world for a period of seventy-odd years. The French Revolution had the same effect, but the rise of Napoleon I aborted the French Revolution and Napoleon's empire followed mercantilist policies.

Mercantilism made a comeback in the United States and some other countries in the last third of the nineteenth century and the first third of this century. The extreme high tariff policies and anti-union attitude of the Republican Party between 1865 and 1933 represented mercantilism without the use of military force for repression. William Jennings Bryan's famous Cross of Gold speech was a ringing denunciation of this neo-mercantilism.

Adam Smith said labor, not gold, money or land, was the true source and measure of wealth. More importantly, he preached absolute dependence on the law of supply and demand, absolute freedom of trade and that economic balance in society and relative prosperity for everyone would be achieved automatically if industry and trade were completely free of government intervention or manipulation, and of monopolies.

Neither *The Declaration of Independence* nor the Constitution contains a precise economic doctrine. The framers of both were far more concerned with religious, personal and political rights and liberties than economics. What they hated was the tyranny that had been practiced in the colonies by the royal governors and their aristocratic toadies, mainly the wealthy planters. But the majority of the colonists were deeply angered by certain manifestations of English mercantilism that discriminated directly against them.

The New Englanders, who had no staples which England was much interested in buying, were dependent on trading wheat, meat, codfish and lumber with the West Indies for cotton, indigo, sugar, molasses and rum in order to get money and goods to trade for English manufactured products. The Molasses Act of 1733 and the Sugar Act of 1764 passed by Parliament in London attempted to prevent the New Englanders from trading with any but the British West Indies and on British terms. The Molasses Act was circumvented easily by smuggling, but the Sugar Act had teeth and was vigorously enforced.

The southern colonies sold tobacco, lumber, hides, naval stores and a few other staples directly to England. Their grievance was that the London mercantile houses were too greedy, paid poor prices for the imports from America and overcharged inordinately for the manufactured goods they shipped out to the colonies. The British applied mercantilist policy not only to manufactures but to such commodities as tea from China and furs bought from the American Indians. This last angered the poorer colonists and some of the well-to-do who wanted to push steadily westward and take the land from the Indians, whom they considered to be making such poor use of the land they did not deserve to be left in possession of it. The mercantilist English, who were making a great thing of selling the furs all over Europe, sought to protect the Indians and even to wink at their raids on the homes and villages of the colonists.

So, even though they had never heard of Adam Smith, the colonists were inclined to be quite favorable to his free-economy ideas. Most people probably will concede that in theory Adam Smith's economic ideas are ideal and a great many persons believe they *can* work and *have* worked whenever they were honestly tried. The great difficulty with Smith's economics is that applying them requires the overwhelming agreement and cooperation of an enormous majority of the people; but the blunt fact is that many, probably most, persons are reluctant to come to such an agreement and cannot be compelled to do so under modern conditions. Everybody is for the free operation of the law of supply and demand for everyone else, but is very eager to have the government intervene to grant special protections and privileges to his or her personal business and financial interests. Smith's famous statement that the purpose of government is to protect the rich from the poor shows that he sensed very clearly how difficult it would be to get mankind to submit to the ideal, egalitarian, autonomous economic system he was advocating.

From the foregoing it is clear that the economic crises we face today grow out of precisely the same economic issues that divided the Crown and the colonies in 1776. However, few historians believe the economic issues were really what stirred the passions of the colonists to rebellion. The sheer stupidity and hubris of King George and his ministers and their incredible inability to communicate with the colonists was what really forced the issue. And even if the basic issues we face today are the same as those of 1776, they are vastly more complicated now.

Generations of American schoolchildren have studied the conflict between Adam Smith economics and mercantilism in the oversimplified frame of high tariff vs. free trade, with the manufacturing North committed to high tariff and the South, with its plantation economy based on slavery, committed to free trade. Many textbook writers concluded that this had as much to do with bringing on the Civil War as the moral issue of slavery and the political issue of states' rights. Certainly, the Union victory in the struggle did usher in a prolonged era of high-tariff mercantilism for the nation.

But there were more important and more fundamental influences than this conflict between free, autonomous economics and government intervention in the growth of the American economy. Nowadays, it is customary to say firmly that there have been just three great socio-economic goals that have dominated American society:

—The desire to own land.
—The desire to be independent.
—The desire for equal opportunity.

Throughout the colonial era and through more than half the history of the Union, the desire to own land was the overwhelming concern of all Americans. The New World had land in abundance to be had for a song. One had only to survey it, cut down the trees, dig a well, build a cabin and plant a crop. Of course a rather high proportion of those arriving from Europe were in no position to take up land at once. They were bond servants, freed from debtors' prison or ordinary prison, bound to toil for five years as household servants or fieldhands before becoming free, and the black slaves coming from Africa had no prospect at all of becoming landholders.

Not surprisingly, a large percentage of those who were free to take up land and did so, were arrant failures at farming. They were not physically or mentally strong enough for the harsh life. They contented themselves with a little hunting, fishing and trapping and perhaps raising a vegetable garden or existing in summer by gathering wild berries and fruits and stealing from their neighbors. When they were caught, they were promptly hanged. There were hardly any prisons in colonial America. Some shiftless persons worked hard but unintelligently. They would clear land and plant a crop, but because they didn't understand crop rotation or care of the soil, they would quickly wear the land out, then have to move on and clear new land.

Those who were both intelligent and industrious, who had been skilled farmers in Europe and arrived here with a few tools, seeds, animals and a little capital, usually did very well on the newly cleared ground and some got rich in a remarkably short time. The successful colonial couple tended to be a Jack and Jill of all trades. The farmer was his own carpenter, stone and brick mason, well digger, blacksmith, horse shoer, livestockman, teamster, butcher, woodchopper, gunsmith and candlemaker. He also had to know how to row and sail a boat and how to build the boat and cut and sew the sails. His wife and daughters cooked, planted vegetables and fruits and flowers, spun yarn, wove cloth and made garments, house linens and blankets, washed, ironed and cleaned house.

Even if a man was a parson, a doctor, a teacher or a lawyer, he and his family had to do about as many different things as the ordinary farming family, and everybody had to join in the field work, clearing, plowing, weeding, cultivating and harvesting. Of course, the more successful families came to have bond servants, hired hands or black slaves to help. Only in Philadelphia, Boston, New York, Richmond and Charleston were there a few merchants and professional people whose major incomes did not come directly from the ownership of land. French New Orleans also had some such people.

However, there was a large sprinkling in all the colonies and on the frontier of trappers and hunters who got their game on public wilderness lands. Their aspiration was to be independent and fancy free, not tied down to any place. But the desire for land gripped most persons. Even sea captains and fisherman and their wives and children ran little farms, perhaps with the aid of a hired hand, while the husband was away at sea. The great desire for land caused many of the German mercenary soldiers who fought for King George in the Revolution to refuse to return to Europe. They settled in the colonies as laborers and eventually took up land.

In the colonial era, ownership of land was about the only way for the average man without exceptional talents and education to achieve even a small degree of personal independence. Colonial society was just what the term implies—based on inequality, injustice and privilege. Only the rich could vote. Political and economic power was concentrated in the hands of the royal governors and their followers. In the case of New England, the bigoted Puritan clergy ruled. Upward social mobility was open only to the boldest and most unscrupulous of the common people and often could be achieved only by the most brutal exploitation of one's neighbors. Most paths to opportunity were blocked by the entrenched privileged status held by the rich and influential and the prevailing mercantilist system. Accordingly, it is not surprising that the vision of a free, autonomous economy such as Adam Smith advocated began to be perceived on this side of the Atlantic by little people who had never heard of Smith. After the Revolution there was an almost universal push to create such an economy. The war and the weak government under the Articles of Confederation, with the worthless state currencies, caused people to pile up such mountains of debt that a civil war between debtors and creditors seemed imminent.

When George Washington became president he put the nation's financial house in order virtually overnight, and the president and Congress then proceeded to install an economic system for the infant republic that conformed to most of Smith's ideas.

In the past century many Europeans have scoffed at the amazing economic growth of the United States, saying it was not a political or social achievement, but merely the ruthless and often wasteful exploitation of the boundless resources of the newly discovered continent. That is not true. Under the Union, American social and economic philosophy and practices were far more progressive and efficient than those of the Old World in spite of the existence of regressive slavery in the agricultural South. Many of the colonists had begun to perceive the need for a new and more efficient economic order long before the Revolution.

Most of them had no intention of toiling to chop down the forests and fight the Indians and the French Canadians merely to enrich English lords and London merchants. They saw, often in rather simplistic terms, that the future development of this new world depended as much on freedom of individual enterprise as on its vast natural resources. They also perceived the vast extent of the New World's economic potential. They realized, for example, that in opposing the settlement of pioneers in the western Indian lands, the lords and merchants in London were concerned about more than the fur trade. The leaders in London realized that if the colonists settled the region between the Appalachians and the Mississippi they would thereby create a nation and economic entity more powerful than England.

It wasn't very long after the Revolution before the midwest was settled and it wasn't much longer before the young republic began displaying an economic vigor such as the world had never before seen. One of the first areas in which the Americans showed their vast economic power and innovative energy was shipbuilding and maritime trading. In the era before railroads and highways, coastal ships necessarily carried most commerce, and American ships were well designed (they were not well built, as a rule; too much green wood was used) and they were magnificently sailed by young, ambitious and shrewd skippers, hard-fisted mates and tough crews. As soon as the Revolution ended, the Stars and Stripes began to appear in all the harbors of the world and Yankee traders became famous for their keenness.

Early in the nineteenth century and down to the post-Civil War era, American sailing ships were the fastest vessels on the oceans and the United States enjoyed a commanding position in the world's maritime trade. This did not last because it was based too much on speculative profit—a new clipper ship sometimes paid for itself and yielded an enormous profit in only two voyages. With the advent of the steamship and regular liner service and fairly economical tramp ships, the profit in such speculation dried up, and so did the American advantages of low ship-building costs and high-speed sailing. But American contributions to the art of ocean navigation were most significant. A young American naval officer, Matthew Fontaine Maury, was the first to study ocean currents scientifically and chart the major currents that traverse the globe, and it was the American, Robert Fulton, who proved the steamship could be made to pay in spite of the cost of coal.

The development of the railroad ended most of the young nation's dependence on coastal and river ships and had the additional importance of reducing dependence on export trade, making the cultivation of the vast home market more attractive. The railroad also was a great spur to mining, heavy manufacturing and large-scale farming.

The first big business men in America were the planters: of tobacco in the Carolinas and Virginia, cotton in the deep South and grains in the North. Fur traders like the Astors and land speculators, including the Astors and Robert Morris (the Philadelphia banker whose failure ruined a number of prominent families), came next, along with the great New England shipping magnates. Railroad tycoons like the Vanderbilts; textile manufacturers; makers of heavy goods such as farm implements, railroad equipment and industrial tools; those who developed the mining of coal, iron and other minerals; and developers of livestock grazing and meat packing also achieved fortunes. Banking developed early and American commercial banks provided funds and services more cheaply than the old-line London merchant banks had. Insurance was a natural outgrowth of this expansion of industry and trade.

Of course, the Louisiana Purchase, the acquisition of Florida and ultimately the war with Mexico, which expanded our lands to the Pacific, accelerated the growth enormously. The territorial expansion brought new floods of land-hungry immigrants from Europe and it brought a new kind of person who did not want to farm but hoped, without owning land, to achieve a financial and personal independence not possible in the country he or she had left. These immigrants were skilled and semi-skilled artisans and even illiterate laborers. They exemplified the second of the great American aspirations—the desire to be independent, to own a small business or to practice a trade or craft as one pleased.

The wide acceptance in the United States of Adam Smith's doctrine that the government should not restrain or intervene in business created a climate highly favorable to the advancement of science and inventions, much more favorable than was possible under the economic climate in continental Europe or even in Britain. Many countries, especially Britain, produced great inventions and much practical science, but in the Old World there was a surprising lack of conscious feeling of urgency about the need for scientific progress.

An example of this can be seen in the writings of Edward Gibbon, author of the monumental *Decline and Fall of the Roman Empire*. The industrial revolution was shaking Britain to its foundations during Gibbon's active life, yet he seems never to have noticed it. His writings indicate he imagined British society would go on unchanged in its stratified structure as it had in the previous century and a half.

The ability to invent things and put innovations to work for the common good is one of the most decisive tests of a nation. Considering that the United States is only a bit over two hundred years old, we measure up extremely well by this test. In the nineteenth century we were long on inventions but not so great in basic scientific research. In this century we have done very well in both. Fulton's steamship and Eli Whitney's cotton gin were the first great American innovations. Whitney was a quite energetic and imaginative man; he also greatly improved the making of gunpowder and contrived many other useful inventions.

Fulton's great achievement was not so much in adapting the steam engine to the ship, but convincing skeptics it would pay to do so instead of relying on the free winds. There were three other great American inventions that advanced ocean transport: John Ericsson's screw propeller and the gyrostabilizer and gyrocompass, both by Elmer Sperry.

Railroads and automobiles were first developed in Europe and so was the diesel engine, but George Westinghouse's airbrake made rail and ultimately highway cargo transportation much safer and more practical. Wilbur and Orville Wright flew the first successful airplane at Kitty Hawk, North Carolina, in 1903, and the U.S. aircraft industry has maintained technological superiority ever since in commercial planes and in military aircraft when needed. The helicopter also is an American development. But, as mentioned previously, right now we are losing ground in aircraft; the French have taken the lead in the helicopter market and the European airbus consortium is making headway in the airliner market.

In farming and harvesting machinery, we have led the world for many years. Cyrus McCormick's invention of the grain reaper and the Rust brothers' cotton picker were the most important American farm machinery inventions, but American companies have invented several thousand other ingenious and complicated machines that have made farming about the least labor intensive industry in the country and have increased production of food and fibers per acre many fold. Except in England, it wasn't until the late 1920s that American-style mechanized farming began to make headway in the Old World.

In horticulture and agricultural chemistry, the United States also has maintained an extremely high rank—number one in the world in most areas of these two fields. George Washington Carver, who was born in slavery, astonished the whole world by developing hundreds of useful products from the sweet potato and the peanut. Luther Burbank, the greatest American horticulturalist, did prodigious things with fruits.

The processing and preservation of foods of all kinds so they could be marketed over considerable periods of time and distributed over large areas without loss is a field of American innovative achievement that would take several large books to describe.

Communications has been one of the greatest areas of American inventive genius. Starting in the 1840s with Samuel F.B. Morse's magnetic telegraph, the United States also produced high speed printing with rotary presses, mechanical typesetting with the linotype and monotype, Alexander Graham Bell's telephone, the first easily used cameras, the phonograph, motion pictures, instant photography and photocopying machines.

An English physicist discovered the waves in nature that are made use of in broadcasting, and the Italian, Guglielmo Marconi, invented wireless telegraphy to use them, but it was the American, Lee DeForest, whose vacuum tube made transmission of the voice and music and, ultimately, images possible. The other two essentials of television, the cathode ray picture tube and the FM circuit, also are American inventions.

The two climactic inventions of this century, the marvelous electronic computer and solid state electronics, which between them have revolutionized nearly all human activity, also are American. It was the transistor and other solid state electronic devices that led to the extreme miniaturization of the computer and so many machines that can be operated electronically. Possibly the most dramatic example of this is the almost total elimination of hot type and even of Ottmar Mergenthaler's marvelous linotype by the printing industry in favor of computerized typesetting and planographic printing from plates produced by photography.

The most prolific of our inventors, of course, was Thomas A. Edison. He was not a scientist and not a terribly good businessman, but he was a marvelously energetic inventor. The electric lamp, practical electric motors and generators, the phonograph and motion pictures were his great achievements, although the Pathé brothers in France invented motion pictures simultaneously and independently of Edison. Edison also had a number of mining and other industrial processing machines to his credit.

Among other important American inventions were the microphone by Emile Berliner; the typewriter by Christopher Sholes, Carlos Glidden and Samuel Soulé; the submarine cable by Cyrus Field; the vulcanizing process by Charles Goodyear; celluloid photographic film by George Eastman; the sewing machine by Elias Howe; the adding machine by William Burroughs; also the ice making machine by Dr. John Gorrie of Florida; and bakelite and nylon, the grandparents of today's huge family of plastics.

In medicine and pharmaceuticals, Dr. Crawford Long in rural Georgia first used ether in 1842 to prove that general anaesthesia can be totally effective in surgery. Following up on the laboratory work of a Cuban scientist, Dr. Walter Reed proved at the turn of the century that both yellow fever and malaria are spread by the bite of the female anopheles mosquito. The Pfizer Company of Brooklyn discovered how to mass produce the anti-biotic penicillin, which had been a laboratory curiosity. Scientists at Rockefeller University in New York and other institutions unraveled the mysteries of the building blocks of living creatures and how their structure is controlled by genetic coding.

The day of the individual inventor probably is almost over in all countries. Inventions nowadays usually come from large teams of scientists, engineers, laboratory technicians and marketing experts, but this is not wholly the case. Individuals and small companies rather than big corporations or government or university laboratories still often are responsible for the most important breakthrough discoveries and inventions. But in pharmaceuticals, chemicals, electronics and big machinery, most patents nowadays are issued for refinements of design rather than basic breakthroughs. And some American industries, notably automobiles, have not fared well in this kind of improvement since the early 1960s, probably for the reasons cited by Professors Hayes and Abernathy.

A complete account of American inventive achievements would fill quite a library. Britain, France, Germany and Japan probably are the only countries that can come close to our overall technological achievements, although in pharmacy and chemistry the Germans have accomplished more than we have.

Yet, just as David Ben-Gurion observed that solving human problems was more important than agricultural or industrial achievements in developing the nation and state of Israel, so men and women have been more important than inventions and technology in our history. This is true mainly because exceptional human beings were responsible for the technology, but men who were totally lacking in inventive or technological skills themselves have also played huge roles in our development. Some, the elder J. Pierpont Morgan and the original John D. Rockefeller, for example, were at times excoriated as robber barons but their vast energies and unbounded optimism served the American people extremely well, and, in the final analysis, they turned out to be extremely public spirited. Other rich men like Jay Gould and Jim Fisk were mere predators, but Bernard M. Baruch, who made his personal fortune by a predatory cornering of the grain market, also was a creative genius with a mind like an electronic computer, who understood, as virtually no one else did, the intricacies of our basic industries; he was called on to marshal these resources and vastly accelerate their output both in World War I and World War II.

Morgan was a banker and a neomercantilist for the most part, but he also had much respect for Adam Smith and a love for his country. He too had a mind like a computer. He attended one of the more famous German universities and majored in mathematics. On graduation he was asked to stay in Germany and teach, but he decided to come home and become a banker. Pilloried frequently in the liberal press as a predatory gambler, the truth is that Morgan always was the constructive builder and such an eternal optimist that he unhesitatingly put his reputation, his business and his personal fortune on the line, on one occasion to force through loans that rescued the U.S. Treasury from collapse.

But the wealthy businessmen who had the greatest impact and shook America most were Andrew Carnegie and Henry Ford. Of course, some of our presidents had great impact on the country's economy—Franklin Delano Roosevelt with his New Deal in the 1930s and Theodore Roosevelt with his trust busting crusade in the first decade of this century, for example—but Carnegie and Ford did more.

Carnegie was a Scot, the son of a weaver. His parents were Chartists, followers of a mildly radical British labor movement. When the power loom ruined his business, the elder Carnegie brought his family to America and settled near Pittsburgh. Young Andy began work at fourteen as a bobbin boy in a textile mill, then became a telegraph messenger and telegrapher. Rather early he landed a job as secretary to the Pittsburgh division manager of the Pennsylvania Railroad, and when his boss went to Washington as transportation director for the Union armies in the Civil War, young Andy went along. He met enough important men and learned enough to prepare himself for a meteoric career, rising steadily in the railroad's service. He invested in a company that made sleeping cars and introduced the first sleepers on the Pennsy's lines. But his greatest business achievement was the early realization that steel, then relatively scarce, was destined to replace cast and wrought iron in virtually all machinery and construction. He went to England to see the inventor, Henry Bessemer, and acquired American rights to Bessemer's steelmaking technology.

Returning to Pittsburgh, Carnegie and several associates started a steel mill that eventually grew into the vast empire which he sold at the turn of the century to a syndicate headed by J. Pierpont Morgan, who renamed it United States Steel Corporation.

Carnegie already had given away a large part of his vast personal fortune, and had written a book entitled *The Gospel of Wealth*, which, although it is not read much today, had a most profound impact on American society. Carnegie was a very religious man and in his book he proclaimed the doctrine that a rich man can justify the accumulation of a vast fortune only by giving it away for the advancement of mankind. He then tried to give away all his estate, which amounted to about $1 billion (which would be at least $8 billion in today's money) and almost succeeded before his death in 1919. He created libraries, gave to many existing libraries, created the Carnegie Foundation for International Peace and a host of other enterprises and funds that gave to colleges and universities, hospitals, research foundations and all aspects of public welfare. There was no American income tax in his day so he was not giving money away to avoid taxes. He married late and had little family to provide for. He was an enlightened but paternalistic man and a somewhat naïve optimist who really believed his peace foundation could put an end to war. The outbreak of World War I shocked him so deeply that he spent his remaining years as a recluse. His influence on American business was that of a master entrepreneur and pioneer in appreciating the need for being far out in front in technology and the recruiting of able people and winning their loyalty and devotion. But the example he set as a philanthropist had an even greater impact. Other rich Americans had been rather liberal in their gifts to charities, community enterprises and education. But after Carnegie's example even the most tight-fisted did not care to risk public criticism from press and politicians or the disapproving stares of their neighbors by not giving generously.

So Andy Carnegie's great contribution to our development was his enlightened Scotch conscience.

Carnegie's influence was reinforced by the views of the great American economist Thorstein Veblen, whose major book, *The Theory of the Leisure Class,* appeared in 1899. The idea of the desirability of an upper class that didn't work for a living depended on the view that these people provided the capital and the high consumption market to create jobs for ordinary mortals, and that these upper-crust individuals, not being buffeted by the daily tides of trade and the sordid pressures of competition, had the leisure to read a lot and provide society with an enlightened, objective leadership. There was a relatively large leisure class in America in Veblen's day and he ridiculed these upper-class idlers mercilessly, especially for their "conspicuous consumption," which he denounced as economic waste aggravated by moral and intellectual stultification. Veblen despised the Republicans of the McKinley era with their neomercantilist policies, but he had no faith that Americans ever would follow Adam Smith's economic ideas consistently enough to let them work freely and efficiently.

We don't have to look around us very widely today to see that a new kind of leisure class has sprung up in the United States out of the affluence of the 1950s and 1960s and, if anything, these new rich of the 1970s and 1980s are more fond of wasteful conspicuous consumption than the generation Veblen castigated.

The conspicuous consumption of these new rich contributes significantly to inflation because it is mostly waste, and waste is inflation by definition. The new rich also commit an economic sin Veblen's leisure class did not even envision—wholesale tax evasion. There was no income tax when Veblen wrote *The Theory of the Leisure Class;* all taxes then were assessed against property or consumption in the form of excise levies.

Today most members of the new leisure class profess to be employed—often both spouses profess to be employed—and they *do* have income from their employment, but their occupations tend to be self-employment which, upon examination, turns out to be mainly a device for sheltering investment and other income from lawful taxation. The bookkeeping losses of farming, cattle grazing, horse ranching, operating art galleries, publishing ventures and hundreds of other operations and investments, including being a minister in some small unheard of religious denomination or operating an allegedly non-profit charitable or welfare foundation, are grossly inflated and used to offset taxable income that must be reported. By diminishing government revenues, this also contributes significantly to inflation, and by diverting capital from more useful purposes it helps contribute to money shortages and high interest rates.

Wiping out virtually all tax shelters might go a long way toward solving our present problems.

Although he was a member of the leisure class himself, President Theodore Roosevelt joined gleefully in Veblen's attack on the idle rich. Teddy worked hard all his days and urged all Americans to follow what he called "the strenuous life." He said the people of the leisure class were too selfish, too anti-intellectual and trivial minded to be useful to society. He said Americans of his own social class bored him almost to tears.

The American who really shook up the economic system and society in the world at large was Henry Ford. Born on a farm in what now is Dearborn, Michigan, he worked as a machinist for a gas lighting company in Detroit and became fascinated with the new gasoline engine. He got into the business of building racing cars and was fortunate enough to acquire the services of the daredevil driver, Barney Oldfield, so was very successful. He then began building passenger cars, one at a time by hand. The automobile of the time, around 1903, was a summer toy of the rich, usually chauffeur driven and maintained. Ford conceived the idea of a car everyone could buy, drive the year around and maintain himself. In accomplishing this, he achieved the greatest transformation of western society since the industrial revolution, with the United States leading the rest of the world by a large margin.

First Ford redesigned the automobile to get the price down, then he redesigned it again so it could be maintained by anybody with a small box of common tools. Finally came the most brilliant idea of all—mass production on an assembly line instead of building the cars one at a time. This enabled Ford to get the basic price of his famous Model T touring car down from $995 to under $350 in five years and to sell fifteen million of the cars in twenty years. That put America on wheels and this forced so many changes in industry, business and social outlook that the whole world was changed.

Naturally, Ford's success influenced the rest of the automobile industry to copy his methods, cut prices and increase production dramatically. Very early, Ford electrified the country by introducing the first five-dollar-a-day factory wage. That was only 15 to 20 percent above prevailing wages but it seemed enormous in those days of rather stable living costs.

Ford's mass production revolution soon spread to other manufacturing with equally dramatic results and its indirect consequences were spectacular. Let's look at some of them:

—It destroyed a twenty-five-hundred-year-old horsedrawn transportation and farming system in much of the world.
—It forced the federal government and the states to build a vast network of paved highways.
—It converted the rubber industry into a giant overnight.
—It created the oil industry as we know it today. In 1908, the oil industry was big but far from holding a dominant position in the economy. Kerosene still was its principal product. Gasoline was almost given away.
—It gave tremendous lift to the steel, electrical, glass, leather, paint and other industries.
—It created the consumer installment financing business that is so huge today.
—It vastly expanded the property/casualty insurance business.
—It greatly improved the resort and tourist industries.
—It made possible a great dispersal of industry from the big cities to smaller communities because it made it easy to get supplies and workers to rural plants and to distribute the products of those plants.
—By making us a mobile nation, it changed our entire outlook.

Of course, some of these changes had their price. Ultimately the automobile revolution Ford created destroyed much of the country's local public transport. We feel this loss today. Some psychologists and historians tend to the view that Ford's revolution has made us too dependent on the automobile and on cheap motor fuel and ultraexpensive highways. Very early in the Ford revolution, some clergymen and social scientists complained that by making us an almost completely mobile nation, Henry Ford had caused us to pull up our roots, destroying the familial and moral foundations of our society.

If any of this criticism ever bothered Henry Ford, he

didn't let on it did. He was not a particularly reflective man, but he was a complicated man with some strong and rather unreasonable prejudices. In his younger years he was a vigorous and outspoken anti-Semite. He was rather anti-intellectual and shocked the academic world by saying bluntly that "history is bunk." He hated politicians but tried unsuccessfully to become one himself. He was sued by his original partners, including the Dodge brothers, and had to disgorge some fifteen million dollars in profits he wanted to hoard for expansion. The court decided Ford Motor Company was so profitable that it could expand and pay the dividends the other partners were demanding. Henry eventually bought the Dodges out. Events justified the court's decision.

Ford was contemptuous of all aesthetics. He didn't care what his cars looked like so long as they performed the way he wanted them to, and he thought it hugely funny to remark that Model T buyers "could have any color they wanted so long as it was black." The surprising thing is that, in spite of Old Henry, early Ford cars usually were rather attractive in appearance.

Ford hated Wall Street so much that Ford Motor Company stock was not made available to the public until long after his death. He hated bankers so much that he kept millions of dollars in currency in his vaults not earning a penny in interest just because he couldn't bear the idea of the bankers making anything on his money.

Like Andrew Carnegie, he was dead set against unions. The great irony is that because they were so successful, Carnegie and Ford created such rising expectations among factory workers that it was they more than anyone else who made the ultimate unionization of American factory workers inevitable.

In the 1920s Ford ignored such technological advances as balloon tires, four-wheel brakes and more comfortable suspension systems and refused to replace the cheap but inconvenient planetary transmission with a gearbox. All these things were rectified with the introduction of the famous Model A in 1927, but many critics thought the Model A should have come two or three years earlier.

As early as 1915, Ford attracted the imagination of the

whole world when he assembled a shipload of fellow pacifists and took them to Europe to try to persuade the Kaiser
and the other heads of the warring states to make peace.
The rulers received him politely but did not listen to him.

Once the United States got into the war, Ford turned
some of his plants into making vehicles and munitions for
the military and demonstrated that he still had his magic
touch by mass producing a small cheap farm tractor that
helped greatly to enable American farmers to feed the Al-
lied armies during the war and hungry Europe after the
peace.

It may be contended that Ford's achievements were so
logical and obvious that someone else would have come up
with them soon if he had not, but it was Ford who *did*
come up with them and, in doing so, gave the United
States such a big economic lead over the rest of the world
that we held it for half a century. The question sometimes
asked is why didn't the revolution Ford ushered in prevent
the great depression that began in October, 1929? There
can be no readily acceptable answer to this question. Historians and economists still are debating the causes of the
Great Depression, and about all they can agree on is that it
was caused by a wide variety of business and government
errors in many countries.

But great as were the contributions of men like Edison,
Carnegie and Ford to the American miracle, there was another aspect equally important—the managerial revolution
and the development of managerial education. Edison's inventions had to be put to work by others for the most part.
When the great man launched a business enterprise on his
own it inevitably came to grief after some initial success.
In spite of his enormous achievements, some of Henry
Ford's business policies made sound professional managers shudder.

The managerial revolution was not an exclusively American phenomenon, but the broad-scale development of
managerial education was unique to America for a long
time. Europeans put a greater emphasis on general education for business and professional men than Americans did,
but they did not create professional management schools

like the University of Pennsylvania's Wharton School,
Dartmouth's Tuck School or the Harvard Business School.
The higher educational systems of Britain and the continental European countries were elitist and tended to perpetuate "old school tie" management classes or at least a
high degree of stultifying intellectual snobbishness in
management.

By definition, the managerial revolution was the re-
placement of hereditary and elitist management by skilled
professionals, and veritable armies of these professionals
were needed to cope with the economic and industrial
changes and expansion growing out of the Ford revolution.
The United States, with its dual system of state supported
and privately endowed universities and colleges, not only
turned out vastly more college graduates per million in-
habitants than any other country, but its educational leaders also were flexible enough to welcome the business
school as a useful addition to the standard university colleges, and American business was swift to see the advantages in this and contribute liberally to the endowments of
the new business schools. The state legislatures soon followed suit, providing funds for business colleges in most
state universities.

In a famous speech at Millsaps College in Jackson, Mississippi, in 1967, Robert McNamara, then U.S. Secretary of
Defense and a former president of Ford Motor Company,
said, "God is clearly democratic, he distributes brainpower
universally but he quite justifiably expects us to do something effective and constructive with that precious gift."

McNamara went on to describe the in-depth development of American managerial education and to ascribe our
then overwhelming position of economic power in the
world to this vast army of well-educated managers. On the
other hand, he said, Europe then was weak in general education, weak in technical education and particularly weak
in managerial education. He also said society cannot survive and develop unless management continues to make
progress.

That was in 1967, at the height of our past economic glory. Harvard Professors Hayes and Abernathy now tell us

that management not only is not continuing to make progress but that it is retrogressing horribly, and it is the faculties of our finest university business schools who are to blame; they have strayed from the path of sound common sense and are teaching shoddy doctrines to the young MBA students who are leading corporations astray and, as the two professors put it, managing the nation into economic decline.

This reminds us of one of Winston Churchill's more famous remarks. In the late 1940s he accused the Labor Party statesmen of war-weary Britain of frittering away things built up with great care and pains over the previous two centuries. For the past decade it must have seemed to many in the world that we Americans have been frittering away things built up with great care and pains by our forebears in the past century.

Let's take a look at where we stood in the world in 1967, and consider what we are losing or have already lost:

—Sixty of eighty-seven companies in the western world with sales exceeding $1 billion a year were American.

—American companies averaged sales gains of 10 percent a year against 7 percent for European companies. Japanese companies were just starting to count.

—General Motors alone earned more than the combined profits of the ten biggest companies in Britain, Germany, France and Japan. With 750,000 workers, General Motors earned as much as forty European and Japanese companies with 3.5 million workers.

—American company profits increased from 7.7 percent of the Gross National Product to 9.5 percent in five years, while the profits of British and French companies based on their GNPs, were almost halved in the same years.

—In most of the 1960s, American companies financed most of their capital investment expenditures out of internally generated funds without borrowing. It was Europe that suffered from high interest rates in 1967, not us.

—American productivity in relation to capital investment was going up sharply every year and we were producing far more goods on less capital per worker than we had back in the 1920s.

At the start of the 1970s, the United States was producing one-third as much manufactured goods and commodities as all the rest of the world put together, with only 6 percent of the world's population and 7 percent of the world's land. Our total output was double that of western Europe and two and a half times that of the Soviet Union.

We were consuming one-third of the world's output of energy and had one-third of the world's highway mileage. Three of every five passenger cars in the world and two of every five trucks operated on our roads. We were producing 73 percent of the world's oil, 70 percent of the globe's machinery, 68 percent of all electronic equipment, and 62 percent of all the chemicals. We flew by far the greatest air mileage of any nation. American labor was 40 percent more productive than Swedish labor, the next highest in the world, and way above the productivity of labor in other European nations and Japan.

Possibly our edge then was a little too big. One of Adam Smith's famous dicta was that the only hope for lasting peace in the world is the achievement of rough economic equilibrium among the nations.

It is now President Reagan's goal to halt the erosion of our economic power and vigor and to put us back on the path of efficiency, growth and strength. This must be done by every one of us, but we are dependent on the White House for leadership, and it is to Ronald Reagan's character, determination and charisma that we must look for this leadership.

This brings us to the last of the three great goals that have dominated American minds throughout our history—the desire for equal opportunity. Many thoughtful observers say that this has become the real frontier and possibly the final frontier of the American dream. Small farming no longer is profitable enough to make ownership of land attractive, although a home is presently a good investment if it can be financed. The proliferation of huge corporations and the vast growth of national, state and local government have not destroyed the desire of people to be independent, but certainly the opportunities have been limited.

So equality of opportunity, particularly educational opportunity, now is vital to all of us, but especially to blacks and other ethnic minorities. Cornell Maier, the energetic and public-spirited chairman of Kaiser Aluminum & Chemical Corporation, recently said that, for the long pull, this is the most important need facing Americans, more important than conquering inflation and high interest rates.

But we won't be able to achieve equality of educational opportunity if we don't hold down inflation permanently and get high interest charges reduced.

In looking at some of the glories of our economic past that we have lost or are losing, I don't want to give the impression that I long for a return to "the good old days." Anybody who lived through the so-called "good old days," will tell you fervently, "They were terrible—you can have them." And often they *were* terrible times, filled with diseases that now have been conquered, poverty so extreme its like is not seen nowadays, monstrous injustice and pervasive ignorance. But our satisfaction in having triumphed over these evils should not make us smug and complacent, it should not blind us to our present grave sins of commission and omission.

IV

The Voices of Babel

SOMETIME AFTER THE DELUGE the descendants of Noah, according to the Bible, tried to build a tower at Babel (the Hebrew name for Babylon), that would reach all the way to Heaven.

But God regarded this as a great presumption, so he suddenly caused the people working on the marvelous tower to speak different languages. They could not understand each other or work together, so the building of the tower stopped. This failure to understand and agree on important matters has been going on in the world ever since. For many centuries the chief voices of dissension and therefore the chief obstacles to the building of a tower to Heaven, obviously an allegorical term for Paradise on earth, were the clergy and the theologians.

Today the chief voices of dissension are those of the economists, who, according to the British economist, Joan Robinson, are the successors to the theologians. She adds that "the solutions offered by the economists are no less delusory than those of the theologians they displaced."* She then contends that nothing very good is likely to happen in the world from the economic point of view until the

*Economic Philosophy by Joan Robinson, Anchor Books, Garden City, N.Y., 1964.

economists stop talking at cross purposes and try seriously
to behave like natural scientists. No economist now will
make the claim that economics is a science.

Even if economics were a science, it is quite certain that
we would not be able to use it to control the economy of a
whole country. Agriculture has become a fairly precise science, but that does not enable man to cope with the vagaries of the weather and obtain consistent crop yields.

President Reagan has to deal with the voices of Babel
continuously. So do all the other rulers in the world, and to
tell the truth it is a good thing that they do, since harmony
is a delightful ideal to contemplate but is deadly to progress most of the time. About the only thing it is valuable
for is in the prosecution of a war, and since we are in a war
against inflation and high interest rates, we could use some
harmony now.

Of course, many people will disagree with this somewhat simplistic analogy of our present precarious situation
to that of Noah's descendants. They will insist, for example, that it is manifestly unfair to give theologians and
economists credit for creating all the confusion and stupidity in the world. What about the earnest efforts in this direction of all the rest of us, the scholars, the philosophers,
the politicians, the poets, novelists, playwrights and journalists and, last but far from least, the businessmen? The
businessmen have planted as much ignorance and confusion as anybody else. If you don't believe that, just read the
Wall Street Journal, any good business magazine or the
business pages of your favorite daily newspaper fairly regularly for a while.

However, there is a way to get a little order out of the
modern voices of Babel. The rabble of real thinkers, moun-
tebanks and loudmouths who write and speak about socio-
economic problems can be sifted and classified to portions
that can be comprehended. The motivations, qualifications
and personalities of these people need not concern us. All
we really want is a digest of their ideas and attitudes so we
can decide which, if any, of them can be helpful in getting
us out of the mess we are in.

According to Professor Robert B. Carson of the State

University of New York at Oneonta,* only three sets of
these ideas need be examined: those of conservatives, liberals and radicals, and he has obligingly proceeded to
present them. It would be pleasant to state that Professor
Carson has found a solution to our problems by means of
his analyses, but, in the conclusion to his book, he flatly
refuses to present any solution or even to say which of the
three conflicting ideologies he personally favors. He de-
nies that that is a cop out; he says that he does have an
opinion but to reveal it would be to destroy the objective
value of his book.

Of course the division of current economic thought into
conservative, liberal and radical camps did not originate
with Professor Carson; everybody talks about conservatives, liberals and radicals but practically no one can give
us a satisfactory definition of any of them. We consider Adam Smith a conservative but he called himself a radical,
which certainly adds zest to the remark of some wit of the
past that "conservatives are persons who worship long
dead radicals."

However, the more one reads Professor Carson and other
academic economists who strive greatly for objectivity, the
more it becomes clear that, at least in the eyes of the radicals, there is a fourth attitude, that of big business, which is
not concerned with economics or social problems at all,
only with profits.

Over all, the three basic modern economic attitudes are:

—Conservative: Depression and protracted economic stagnation are not natural consequences of capitalist economic
practices.
—Liberal: Only vigorous countercyclical government intervention can control a natural propensity of the capitalist
economy towards recession and depression.
—Radical: Recurrent crises never can be prevented so
long as the goal of production is profit instead of human
needs.

Macroeconomic Issues Today, by Robert B. Carson, St. Martin's Press,
New York, 1980.

Perhaps one gets the clearest view of how these three philosophies look at specific socio-economic questions by seeing how differently conservatives, liberals and radicals look at proposals for national economic planning. We are talking now about large-scale overall national planning such as the communists employ in Russia, China and Cuba, and such as the fascists employed in Germany and Italy.

The radical view is the most revealing. The radicals are much more against national economic planning than the conservatives are but for vastly different reasons. The radicals simply see national economic planning as a means of preserving the growth of corporate profits at any cost, even at the price of enslaving all the people except the very rich. The radicals say capitalism has exhausted its possibilities under free enterprise economics and therefore needs total national economic planning in order for big business's management and stockholders to survive. They claim that this is not new, that it would be only a repetition of the way the Republican Party forced high tariffs, low wages and restricted civil rights on the nation in the seventy years following the Civil War.

Professor Carson observes that, as the radicals see matters, "the crowning irrationality of the system [capitalism] is that it can produce more and more but labor becomes increasingly redundant and markets harder to find." The radicals believe that big business, in spite of the lip service it gives to free enterprise ideas, will resort to brutal government intervention through national economic planning in order to reintroduce the "iron law of wages" of the 1600s and 1700s, the doctrine that wages must never be allowed to be more than enough to provide the workers with a bare subsistence, because profits for the proprietors of business are sacred, and any wage above the subsistence level threatens profits too much.

The positive side of the radical view is expressed by radical economist William Appleman Williams* who argues

*The Great Evasion, by William A. Williams, Quadrangle Books, Chicago, 1964.

that the only long-range solution to our problems is to decentralize the national economy and rebuild society without "the confining limits of property and destructive dynamics of the competitive market place."

But we have seen these radical ideas put in practice in the Soviet Union for sixty-five years and they have not produced a paradise. They have spread to other countries as a reaction to the destruction of war, but they have not created any miracles.

The conservative attitude on this question of national economic planning is based to a considerable extent on the early and continuing failures and absurdities of Soviet planning. The conservatives see the adoption of national economic planning as the end of free enterprise society and the creation of a dictatorship that would be inherently inefficient. They deny the accusation of the radicals and liberals that the free market is anarchistic. They point out that a market operates like a machine and a machine's operation has to be planned, but contend that this kind of market planning has no resemblance to overall bureaucratic planning.

The Chicago conservative economist, Milton Friedman, puts it rather bluntly, saying the choice is between "the voluntary cooperation of individuals, the technique of the marketplace" or "central direction involving the use of coercion—the technique of the army and the modern totalitarian state."*

The curious thing here is that we see the two opposite poles of opinion both raising the spectre of dictatorship based on military force. The conservatives fear Lenin's "dictatorship of the proletariat" and the radicals fear dictatorship of a selfish financial oligarchy that doesn't care a damn about either people or ideology.

In between stand the liberals who cling to the belief that good national economic planning could make our present mixture of Adam Smith and Keynesian (pro-government-intervention) economics work a lot better and provide the

Capitalism and Freedom, by Milton Friedman, University of Chicago Press, 1976.

stability needed to create a lot more jobs. Their view is that "the quaint little world of Adam Smith" perished a long time ago (Professor Carson asks if it ever really existed) and that conservative defenders of individualism and freedom have failed to adapt their views and values to a highly complex technological world.

It goes without saying that the people represented by each of these attitudes (and by the alleged fourth attitude of big business) actually are fragmented into many different shades of opinion and selfish interest, and are rather vociferous, demanding and often unscrupulous in presenting their ideas; therefore, describing them as the voices of Babel is by no means far-fetched.

But history indicates that, up to very recent times at least, the philosophy and economic structures of a nation counted for less in its record of achievement than did the energy, determination, innovative restlessness and overall intelligence and decency of the people. Nations whose socio-economic systems have included the most obvious absurdities and injustices have done well for long periods, while other nations whose social structure seemed idyllic perished because the people were not sufficiently vigorous or intelligent.

Ironically, this three-sided scenario of attitudes toward national economic planning has quite a *déjà vu* sound. Back in the 1930s, the conservatives, the radicals and some of the liberals were raising the same spectre of dictatorship with much more reason, because fascist dictatorships actually had risen in Italy, Germany, Portugal, Spain, Hungary, Romania, Japan and Yugoslavia. (The liberal novelist Sinclair Lewis wrote a novel and a play, entitled *It Can't Happen Here*, about a fascist revolution in the United States.) We survived the threats of the 1930s and the great war that followed them, so we ought to feel that we can survive the divisions expressed by the present voices of Babel.

Popular attitudes in the United States at present do not appear to reflect great fear of dictatorship or iron repression. Yet we cannot be blind and deaf to the murderous repression that has been going on in El Salvador, Guatemala, Iran, Afghanistan, Lebanon, Poland and some other countries. Americans are well aware of the strong element of hypocrisy underlying all ideological postures. The radical elements who clamor the most loudly for decentralization of society are precisely the elements who live on student loans, research grants, public welfare and hold jobs in public institutions made possible by the centralization of society in this century. The conservatives and some of the liberals who are most enthusiastic about free trade and minimal government intervention in the economy are the persons most avidly seeking tax shelters, tax loopholes and special privileges for their particular occupations and businesses.

The postures of the conservatives, liberals and radicals on other public issues, past and present, are interesting. For example, many of the conservatives still contend as they did in the 1932 electoral campaign that the country was emerging from the Great Depression under President Hoover's policies and that a growing fear that Franklin Roosevelt would be elected president aborted the recovery. They do not accept the Keynesian view that there was something unique and non-cyclical about the 1929 collapse. But the conservative economists now concede that the Federal Reserve Board may have made the crisis inevitable by following too tight money policies as a reflex reaction to the great bull stock market of 1928 and 1929. The conservatives say the Fed made a second big mistake by not coming to the rescue of the Bank of the United States in New York City when it failed in December, 1930. The resulting panic caused a lot of banks to fail. A third mistake by the Fed was in raising interest rates in September, 1931, in a moment of fear over an international gold crisis.

The radicals believe the 1929 depression was the result of the failure of real wages to move upward in the 1920s and of the huge and unwise expansion of consumer debt in the 1920s.

We could examine the dramatically varying attitudes of conservatives, liberals and radicals on a variety of socioeconomic issues as Professor Carson does—international trade, stabilization policies of the Nixon, Ford and Carter administrations, and defense outlays, for example—and we

would always come up with much the same basic opinions.
The conservatives would say government intervention
worsened every problem, the liberals would say it helped
things and the radicals would say nothing is going to work
until we abandon the profit motive altogether because the
profit motive inevitably leads to overproduction, the production of socially useless goods and simultaneous under-
consumption in relation to production in order to maximize
profits.

The radical argument is that profitability is no longer an
adequate barometer on which to base economic activity. In
absolute terms and in the short term, this may well be true.
As we already have pointed out, the best run multinational
companies no longer give top priority in their operations to
short-term profit. And that would seem to give the lie to
the radical theory that big business is willing to go the
length of extreme repression and starve people in order to
maximize profit.

Nevertheless, centuries of human experience show that
the profit incentive is the most powerful for nearly all hu-
mans and to try to do away with it always arouses emotional and intellectual opposition.

Freedom of ideas is basic to democracy. The conservatives, liberals and radicals all have the right to express
their views and press for their adoption, but in the end
sound common sense must prevail, and in the United
States today the only way common sense can prevail is by
getting good leadership from the White House. We certainly cannot hope to get it from Congress.

Irregardless of the merits of all his individual policies,
Ronald Reagan has shown us that he is a determined man
and a sensible man who is not likely to be befuddled by
the voices of Babel. He is well aware that on the surface
the political and socio-economic climate of the United
States seems to change with the speed of the images in a
kaleidoscope, but the real verities change very slowly
indeed.

V

The Juggernaut

THE GREATEST OBSTACLE to getting high interest rates down and to keeping the lid permanently shut on inflation is repeated and massive federal government deficits.

In the second half of 1982, President Reagan's long-range program was frustrated by the need for federal borrowing of $85 billion to $110 billion to finance the prospective deficit, and the biggest cause of the deficit was spending on defense.

This has been the case, with the exception of only a few years, ever since the Cold War began soon after World War II. Defense expenditures have a far greater inflationary impact both on price levels and interest rates than other spending because, from the economic point of view, they are totally unproductive.

We had repeated federal deficits in the 1930s but they did not cause inflation or high interest rates. Not even President Franklin Roosevelt's doubling of the official price of gold created any inflation significant enough for people to feel it. There were two reasons for this. In the first place, such price increases as did occur were from the extremely depressed levels of the Hoover depression and, second, the deficit spending was on human needs, not on armaments.

Of course, a lot of our deficit spending in the post-war
era also was on human needs, but much of it was spent not
on basic necessities, but on things our forefathers would
have considered extravagant luxuries and rightly so. Nevertheless, much of the spending did prove productive.
Spending on education enabled us to reach a dominant position in technology, even though a lot of the research
grants were demonstrably wasteful and useless.

We recovered very handily from the inflation brought
about by World War II, only to be thrust in rapid succession into the Cold War, the Korean War and the war in Vietnam, into support of Israel in the Middle East and into providing arms for Latin-American and Asian nations
threatened by communist-supported anarchy.

During Richard Nixon's administration, when the war in
Vietnam was being wound down, there was a lot of talk
about the "peace dividend" that would provide the federal
government with a surplus that could eliminate inflation.
This dividend never materialized for many reasons, one
being the Arab oil embargo of 1973, another the upheaval
in Iran, and the last and perhaps most important, the rather
rapid loss of the managerial and technological edge the
American industrial establishment had enjoyed since the
war. The enormous increase in demand for social benefits
resulting from an unprecedented revolution of rising expectations also aggravated the situation.

The first Arab oil embargo enormously increased the
cost of doing business in all industries and forced government and industry to borrow much more heavily than in
the past.

Thus vanished the peace dividend.

That left us with a monstrous situation, the prospect of
which President Dwight Eisenhower had warned us in the
closing days of his term in the White House—the peril of
having created a military-industrial juggernaut that destroys the national economy with wasteful outlays on un-
necessary and obsolete or obsolescent armaments. By his
blind faith in the Cold War policies of his secretary of state,
John Foster Dulles, Eisenhower virtually committed the
nation to the very peril he was warning against, and Lyn-

don Johnson compounded this error by stubbornly expanding the war in Vietnam without putting the country on a wartime economic footing.

This frightening juggernaut now is with us and is bigger and more monstrous than President Eisenhower ever imagined. It is an arrogant runaway giant that has our Congress, our military and industrial leaders and much of the populace mesmerized. Its wasteful arrogance knows no bounds of authority or common sense. A shocking proposal to spend over $400 million to remodel and reactivate a totally useless and obsolete battleship that would be a sitting duck for land-based or carrier-based enemy missiles is typical of the psychology of the naval and military men and defense contractors who hold the reins of power in our military-defense establishment.

His continued espousal of such conventional defense outlays is the one area in which Ronald Reagan has the most difficulty.

However, the main cause of our crushing and stultifying armaments burden is not of our own making. All Americans know that the real cause is Russian expansionism and aggression. Russia not only has been aggressive and expansionist, but treacherous. Josef Stalin seized the eastern province of Czechoslovakia when Adolf Hitler dismembered the little republic. He attacked and mutilated Finland without provocation in 1939. He made a treacherous treaty with Hitler, leaving the fascist dictator free to overrun all western Europe. He seized control of Estonia, Latvia, Lithuania, Poland, Hungary, Romania, Bulgaria and Czechoslovakia after the war and tried to seize control of China and Korea. His successors tried to seize Cuba and fomented bloody civil wars in Africa, Asia and Latin-America.

So, not surprisingly then, nearly all Americans blame Russia entirely for the continuing Cold War and the burden of maintaining armaments.

Not quite all though. Some radical economists and philosophical leaders among us say war and big armaments budgets simply are a necessary aim of capitalism, that sooner or later every capitalist society has to resort to war to maintain employment and the profit system. These myopic souls maintain that every prolonged period when the United States was at peace became an era of stagnation because of the oppressive nature of capitalism. Fortunately, not many Americans swallow this hogwash. One reason we do not swallow it is because it is easy to observe that the armaments burdens of the communist nations are much greater than ours and they are much quicker to go to war than we are and on far less provocation. The entire world is completely mystified by the brutal Soviet invasion of Afghanistan; it makes no sense at all.

Why are the Russians so warlike?

Historically, this question far antedates Lenin and the 1917 revolution that made Russia communist. We must find the answer to the question if we are ever going to get the monkey of big armament outlays off our backs, and we must start our search for the answer with Napoleon Bonaparte more than a hundred and seventy years ago. The French emperor's arrogant and devastating invasion of Russia in 1812 without any real provocation and against the counsel of many of his own wisest advisors, left a legacy of hatred for the west among the Russian people.

This attitude was hardened by the Crimean War in the middle of the nineteenth century when Britain, France, Turkey and Sardinia invaded Russia on a variety of flimsy pretexts. The war did not have a conclusive result but it again embittered Russians against the west.

Russia's humiliating defeat in the Russo-Japanese war of 1905 further aggravated Russian fear of the west. The Russians felt that the western nations had sympathized with Nippon and helped Tokyo. President Theodore Roosevelt of the United States was called on to mediate a settlement of the war and Teddy's open expression of his contemptuous opinion of the Russians added to their grievances.

In the years preceding World War I many Russians felt that the western peoples looked on them as savages. The view of the great English geographer, Halford Mackinder, which was echoed by Roosevelt, that the Russian nation was a vast time bomb that might some day explode and destroy all civilization also hurt Russian sensibilities.

In World War I the Russians were badly defeated by Germany and Austria and the Germans then cynically sent Vladimir Lenin and his colleagues from Switzerland to Russia to take over the resulting revolution and make a separate peace with the Kaiser. Hindsight reveals that the reaction of the western allies, including President Wilson's of the United States, in sending troops to Russia ostensibly to protect foreigners but in reality to aid the remaining Czarist forces, was a great mistake. It greatly increased Russian distrust of all the west. The diplomatic and economic quarantine imposed on the young Soviet Union in the 1920s by the western nations, especially the United States, was an even greater cause for grievance.

But the greatest base for Russia's paranoid and aggressive attitude was the rise of Adolf Hitler's Nazi empire. From the very start of Hitler's rise to power, Stalin and the rest of the Russians feared that the fury of Nazi aggression would be hurled against them and the western nations would do nothing to prevent it. Stalin tried to prevent it by the Molotov-Ribbentrop treaty, but Hitler cynically repudiated the treaty and waged one of the most brutal and devastating invasions in all history against Russia.

The western nations, particularly the United States, did help the Soviet Union with supplies but, from the Russian point of view, we should have opened a second front up through the Balkans, which had been overrun by the Germans, in order to take some of the pressure off the Russian armies. Ironically, Winston Churchill held the same view but for different reasons. Churchill knew the Russians would win and he did not want them overrunning the Balkans, Hungary, Czechoslovakia and eastern Germany as they ultimately did. President Franklin Roosevelt and his top generals, George Marshall and Dwight Eisenhower, opposed the whole idea of a Balkan front.

It would be a gross oversimplification to say the Russians act as they do solely out of fear, but it is impossible to find any other motive for some of their more glaring aggressions. However, although we accused them of acting irrationally in attacking Finland in 1939 "to close the door to Leningrad," the fact is that the Germans subsequently did attack Leningrad through Finland.

After World War II it seemed to the Russians that the United States had erected a ring of offensive military, naval and air bases around the world all aimed at Russia. Actually most of these bases were set up originally for the containment and destruction of German and Japanese forces and were not aimed at Russia. But the Russian expansionist posture after the war caused the United States to retain these bases instead of abandoning them. Also every petty rightist dictator in the world proceeded to wheedle money and arms out of the United States on the pretext that he needed them for defense against Russian-inspired revolution. Actually what the arms were needed for was to maintain the dictators in power.

What is the lesson for today of this brief look at one hundred and seventy years of history?

Is it not that the real villains in the armaments race are not so much the Russians or the rulers of the west but the ghosts of Napoleon Bonaparte, Kaiser Wilhelm II and Adolf Hitler?

Bumbling, short-sighted modern politicians adopt rigid attitudes that perpetuate the fears and prejudices growing out of the past and make agreement between east and west impossible. The Russians and western leaders are equally guilty of this.

Sincere efforts have been made by many persons since World War II to thaw out these unreasonable and irrational attitudes, but with almost no success; and they have been sidetracked by such setbacks as the Korean war, the war in Vietnam and the many conflicts in the Middle East.

So the American people are left not only with the huge cost of maintaining their own vast military establishment but the necessity of allowing France, West Germany, Italy, Spain, Greece, Israel, Saudia Arabia, India, Pakistan, Japan, Taiwan and many other countries to lean on us heavily for defense, and this vastly aggravates the burden on U.S. taxpayers. It may be argued that the foreign nations pay for the armaments and some of the manpower we provide, but that isn't strictly true; they often only promise to pay and the promises have to be underwritten in the bond markets by American taxpayers.

Certainly our arms production is profitable, but to whom? They may be to the shareholders of some corporations, although most corporate managers claim that, for a variety of reasons, defense business is not nearly so profitable as commercial business. Arms sales are vastly profitable to agents and brokers, both American and foreign, and they are profitable to foreign politicians and to American politicians who seek defense plants for their home districts and benefit from the business either directly through corrupt expenditures or indirectly by creating jobs in their communities and thus perpetuating themselves in office while shifting the huge cost burden to the nation as a whole.

We need to think back to before World War II, which was before most of today's populace was born, in order to realize how heavy the burden of armaments really rests upon us. One of the prime charges against King George III in the Declaration of Independence was that he had quartered large standing armies among us. We demobilized completely after the Civil War, after the war with Spain and after World War I. Our regular army in the mid-1930s was only a little over 100,000 men. There was no Air Force then and the Navy, including the Marine Corps, was only a little larger than the Army. Except for warships, weaponry was relatively unsophisticated. Even military and naval aircraft were not terribly expensive.

We never can go all the way back to those times but if we ever are to solve our problem of stagflation we must go a considerable part of the way back, and going back means coming to a reasonable understanding with the Russians and with the aspirations of emerging nations of the world, whose peoples are tired of being ruled by landed oligarchies and military dictatorships.

The billions of dollars we are spending on military aid to other nations might make a little sense if any of them were the least bit grateful to us or had the slightest intention of fighting for us in case of a showdown, but that is not the case. Their only interest in us is as a source of handouts, a market for their goods, a place to dump their surplus population and a profitable place to invest. The measure of their feelings for us is that their governments resent our high interest rates because they drain capital out of their lands. They refuse to bear their share of what we consider to be the necessary burden of western defense, and if they produce any arms themselves they sell them to governments that are unfriendly to us.

Clearly, most of them do not believe the Russians ever will attack them and they appear to believe that we could blunder and plunge the world into a third World War.

The successive failures of the invasions by Napoleon, Kaiser Wilhelm II and Hitler ought to have convinced the Russians by now that no power on earth can conquer them or even invade them successfully and that, therefore, the adventures they engaged in in recent years in Hungary, Cuba, Afghanistan and Poland are not worthwhile and in the long run are stupid and dangerous. When he was in the White House, Theodore Roosevelt, who did not like the Russians, said that unless she was destroyed by the unrest within her, he did not see how Russia could fail to achieve a position of overshadowing power in the world because of her extremely favorable geographical situation and her enormous potential in people and natural resources.

Of course, the average Russian does not look back some generations to analyze his or her reasons for fearing the west. They have plenty of recent reasons. Russia lost 20 million lives in World War II. So every Russian has a paranoid fear of the Soviet Union being invaded again or attacked from the air with nuclear weapons. Nuclear missiles have put most of Russia within range of such an attack and even though the Soviet Union has tremendous retaliatory capability, the potential of slaughter and destruction is too dreadful to be contemplated.

Russian children have it drummed into them from early childhood that capitalism leads to war and that the ruling classes of all capitalist countries are willing to take their subservient masses into war against the communist world. We have to convince them that this is not true.

There still are strong vestiges of old-fashioned Czarist

pan-Slavic imperialist psychology in Russia, and this undoubtedly is a factor in the irrationality of much Kremlin
policy.

These two last prevailing Russian psychological currents
have caused some western critics of Soviet long-range philosophy to accuse the Russians of wanting to impose a Pax
Sovietica on the modern world the way the Caesars imposed the Pax Romana on the ancient world. The Roman
legions did maintain an uncertain peace in Europe, Asia
Minor and North Africa for several centuries but at the
price of enslavement and social stagnation, and eventually
the Pax Romana was shattered by internal dissensions in
the empire and the invading hordes of barbarians from the
north.

So our logical course of action lies in convincing the Russian people we never will attack them but that we will defend the western hemisphere and perhaps western Europe
if they are attacked. We owe nothing to the rest of the nations of the world. Are we really obligated to defend Japan,
Germany and Italy because we defeated them in a war
they began?

Trying to be the world's policeman is a task too big for
either us or the Russians, as they soon would discover if
they tried it. They have had enough trouble policing the
communist bloc states.

For an excellent reason, borne out by history, we should
desire prosperity in the world for the Russians as we desire
it for ourselves. Generally speaking, nations do not launch
wars when they are prosperous and feel sure of continued
prosperity and stability. Of course this is not always the
case. History is full of wars caused by the blunders of paranoid rulers of prosperous nations, but the peoples themselves do not become warlike until they start to suffer or
feel threatened. It is when times are bad and when danger
seems real and near that it becomes easy for rulers to get
the common people to follow the flag and march bravely
into battle. The enthusiasm displayed by the Iranians in
attacking Iraq in the summer of 1982 was a prime example
of that.

Although solving the problem of our defense burden is,

in the final analysis, a matter of diplomacy and developing goodwill, there is much else we can do on our own to ease the burden. There is nothing more wasteful in the world than a huge military establishment and nothing more lacking in scruples, decency or intelligence. It is inherently wasteful because the first principle of logistics, which means military and naval economics, is that nothing can be measured in terms of monetary cost but only in terms of potential for success and survival.

Wasteful mistakes in defense based on wishful thinking and hubris on the part of military and naval leaders, politicians and defense manufacturers are the rule rather than the exception. This vast waste not only is a burden to taxpayers, it diverts vast sums from useful productive enterprise and is the biggest cause of inflation and runaway interest rates.

Like the battleship, the jumbo aircraft carrier is so vulnerable to land-based missiles and bombing planes and nuclear-powered submarines firing nuclear weapons that it is stupid to depend on them. This was shown by the ship losses the British incurred in the brief Falkland Islands war.

A big defense industry not only is non-productive from the economic point of view, it is intensely cyclical according to the degree of fear prevailing in the nation and hence helps to create boom and bust cycles. Defense industry is capital intensive rather than labor intensive and does not provide nearly as many jobs for the expenditures as most straight commercial business. However, the armed forces themselves admittedly are labor intensive.

Defense also is the most speculative of all businesses— so the taxpayers pay for all the losses. No corporate executive would dare risk his own company's money in the tank, missiles, fighter, bomber, warship or weapons businesses without an absolute guaranty from the government for every penny. Even with such a guaranty, the contractor may make only a very modest profit because the generals and admirals keep changing the specifications, then refuse to pay for all the cost overruns.

Defense industry is largely monopolistic. The submis-

sion of competitive bids is often a rigged farce. This monopolistic nature of the industry makes it hard to fix responsibility for blunders and the temptation to sloth and
corruption is vast as compared to commercial business. No
other industry is so vulnerable to lobbying pressures in
Congress.

Defense spending does produce inventions and innovations that ultimately become useful in civilian industry,
but only at extremely high cost.

Large corporations get most defense contracts, therefore
big defense strengthens big business and tends to make
the nation's business climate less competitive, a monopolistic economy that can become increasingly oppressive for
all of society.

Defense spending in the United States declined from 9
percent of the Gross National Product in 1968, which was
near the peak of the war in Vietnam, to about 4.5 percent in
1978–79, but has risen since and is rising now. In actual
dollar outlays, it dropped from $76.9 billion in 1968 to
$70.2 billion in 1970, but has risen steadily since then be-
cause of price escalation.

In 1939, two years before we entered World War II, our
defense budget was only $1.9 billion, which would be
about $6.65 billion in 1980 dollars as measured by the fed-
eral consumer price index. It jumped to $84.4 billion in
1944, a peak in World War II. That would be almost $300
billion in 1980 dollars. It dropped to $13.2 billion in 1949.
With the high inflation of the Carter administration, it hit
$125 billion in 1978.

Statistics on the relative numbers of men under arms for
the United States and Russia and the numbers of weapons
of each important category are the subject of great international debate. According to figures published by the U.S.
government and the International Institute for Strategic
Studies, the armed forces of the United States declined
from 2.5 million men in 1960–61 to 2.1 million in 1978–79,
while those of the Soviet Union rose from 3.6 million to 4.4
million. The number of American tanks remained station-
ary at 12,500 while Soviet tanks increased from 35,000 to
45,000. The American defense budget (expressed in infla-

tion-adjusted 1979 dollars) fell from $125 billion to $123.7 billion during the Carter administration while the Russian defense outlays rose on the same basis from $91 billion to $162 billion. It was the same relative story in missile-firing submarines and intercontinental ballistic missiles. I give no figures on aircraft because, not only are they unreliable, but many military experts doubt that bombers and fighter planes ever again will play a decisive role in war.

Many years ago someone said the worst trouble with defense spending was that the generals and admirals never prepare to fight the next war, but only to fight the last war over again, and the weapons are nearly always obsolete when they reach the front.

That may not be quite as true now as in the past, but the Falklands fighting showed that war still is full of unpleasant surprises. This brief struggle also showed that good morale and training and good officers and noncoms still win more battles than superiority in numbers or equipment.

That brings us up to the present agitation for a total freeze on nuclear weapons. This agitation clearly is making much headway both in the free enterprise world and in the communist world. Many people want such a freeze without the actual achievement of nuclear parity between the United States and the Soviet Union because they think neither a nuclear edge nor parity can be any assurance of survival to either superpower in case of a showdown.

This all being the case, President Reagan is correct in calling for a strong military posture. He is truly put in the middle, "between the devil and the deep blue sea." He knows we must carry a "big stick."

The overwhelming conclusion then must be that from every point of view big defense spending in peacetime now is prohibitive for any nation.

For one thing, a defense establishment accumulates huge tracts of land and obsolete fortresses and other installations that cost the taxpayers billions unnecessarily. The Wall Street Journal said on July 16, 1982, that American taxpayers were spending $16 billion a year just to maintain and operate some four thousand bases around the world, many of which are totally obsolete and have been for decades. Many of them are kept open because of local "pork barrel" political pressure, others out of foolish devotion to tradition.

Certainly it would seem wise to close many of these bases and sell off the land so it can be returned to productive use in industry, agricultural or residential developments.

VI

Destructive Taxation

RONALD REAGAN says he is determined to ease the tax burden of the American people.

That raises the question of what the tax burden really is. Is it the total amount of money the federal, state and local governments take from our bank accounts and pocketbooks? Is it the way taxes are levied and the resulting distribution of the burden among the rich, the moderately well-to-do and the poor? Or is the way in which taxes affect economic productivity, the rate of savings, the creation of jobs or the driving of people into the underground economy to evade taxation the really disastrous burden?

A moment's reflection will compel us to agree that all these factors are part of the tax burden, but the last may be the really critical issue.

Most of the debate in Congress and among academic economists is over the distribution of the tax burden between the rich and low-income groups. The United States was the first nation in the world to make a great effort to achieve a reasonably equitable distribution of the tax burden between rich and poor. We were not the first nation to adopt the income tax but we were the first to adopt one with sufficient progressive steps to tax the rich proportionately more heavily than ordinary folk. All previous tax systems were based frankly on the old-fashioned feudal and

128

mercantilist philosophy that taxes were mainly meant to be collected from the common people in order to support the king, the aristocracy and the higher clergy in luxury. The aristocrats and rich merchants had other financial obligations to the king; they were required to raise regiments of troops or furnish him with warships at their personal expense, for example, but as Sir Walter Raleigh observed, the nobles and well-to-do of Elizabethan England were taxed on only a sixth to a fifth of their wealth while the common people were taxed on every penny they could scrape together.

In the first hundred and twenty years of our national history, the federal government lived in peacetime largely on excise taxes on liquor, tobacco and a few other things, customs duties on imports and stamp taxes on documents. The states and local governments lived off property taxes on real estate and personal property and poll or "head" taxes for such things as road or school districts.

The federal government imposed special taxes in wartime. During the Civil War these special taxes included an income levy, but the Supreme Court later declared the income tax unconstitutional and it was not enacted permanently until after a constitutional amendment was ratified in 1911.

Things changed drastically after the first income tax was collected in 1913. The income tax speedily became the major source of the national government's revenue and in time most states and a number of cities also adopted income taxes. But until World War II the income tax was almost but not quite entirely a levy on individual incomes. A capital gains tax was added rather soon to tax profit made on the sale of land, securities or other property. Such profits were not considered income because they were not earned as salaries, fees or commissions and were not dividends or interest on investments. Since the capital gains tax schedules have been at lower rates than those on straight income, speculation in properties speedily became a preoccupation of the moneyed classes.

Adoption of the steeply progressive income tax, rigorous

inheritance or estate taxes and the capital gains tax resulted from the growing cost and complexity of the national government and the declining importance late in the nineteenth century and early in this century of imports, so that less revenue was realized from customs duties. The ideas advanced by men like Andrew Carnegie, Thorstein Veblen and Theodore Roosevelt and theories advanced by British economists also were important in bringing about the drastic change in the tax structure.

Teddy Roosevelt's diatribes against "malefactors of great wealth" had much to do with speeding the ratification of the income tax amendment.

From the start, the federal income tax was levied in a small way on corporations but, until just before World War II, the corporate income tax rates were modest. They were intended merely to raise a little extra revenue, not to exercise any influence on the way business was conducted or the way corporations should be managed. The corporate income tax rate started at 1 percent in 1913. It was raised during World War I and reached 13.5 percent by 1926. In 1936, it ranged from 8 to 15 percent.

Meanwhile the individual income tax rates were raised very sharply to finance President Franklin Roosevelt's New Deal policies and this caused many wealthy persons who controlled corporations to use them as tax shelters by having the corporations retain most of their earnings instead of paying them out in dividends to be taxed at individual rates. The retained earnings were taxed only at the much lower corporate rates. Also, they could be reinvested by the corporation to earn additional profits. Not surprisingly there was a great hue and cry against this hoarding of corporate earnings. This, plus the federal government's growing need for big revenues as the rise of Hitler and Japanese imperialism made it imperative for the United States to rearm, resulted in large increases in the corporate income tax rates.

At first it was proposed to impose the higher rates only on retained earnings, but Congress rejected that, raised the rates across the board and added a penalty tax on undistributed profits. This penalty tax on retained earnings proved most unpopular and was repealed after only a couple of years. But the corporate income tax rate went up and up. It hit 40 percent during World War II and reached a peak of 52 percent by 1952 in the Korean war. This big increase did solve the problem of tax avoidance by retaining profits undistributed in closely held corporations; the profits now were taxed about as rigorously as if they had been distributed in dividends. But this raised the problem of double taxation of dividend income at both the corporate and individual rates, which is still with us.

Meanwhile, individual income tax rates moved rapidly up, and during World War II Congress adopted an income withholding tax that made tax evasion almost impossible for most persons on wages and salaries.

The creation of a big corporate income tax had many other consequences that should have been foreseen but were not. A big corporate income tax is totally wrongheaded, and it soon began to distort the entire economy of the nation by influencing business policy and corporate management in wrong ways.

An income levy taxes corporations on their profitability, not on their activity, therefore it follows as night follows day that such a tax unjustly and foolishly penalizes efficient companies that earn a steady profit and rewards inefficient companies that earn very little or lose money. This is sheer idiocy, yet millions of Americans perversely insist on believing in it. Senator William Proxmire of Wisconsin has been campaigning for repeal of the corporate income tax for years, and so have some excellent academic and business economists, but they never get anywhere. Politicians, labor leaders and much of the public simply retort that corporations in general are rich and should shoulder the biggest share of the country's tax burden.

But corporations and unincorporated businesses are heavily taxed even without this idiotic levy on profitability. They pay taxes on land and other property, franchise taxes, license taxes, customs duties, gasoline and other sales taxes, highway and other user taxes, Social Security taxes, workmen's compensation insurance fees and various excise taxes.

Of course, if the corporate income tax ultimately is repealed the revenue it now raises must be replaced in some
manner, but if the corporations are to continue to produce
that revenue they should be taxed on activity, not on profitability; then the tax burden would fall fairly on all companies and would not unjustly penalize the prosperous, efficient businesses.

Another serious flaw of the corporate income tax is that it
helps to price American exports out of world markets. This
is a much more serious matter than it used to be because
our high interest costs and the recent great strength of the
U.S. dollar in the foreign currency markets also are pricing
American goods out of world markets. Countries that need
to increase their export trade, as the United States now
does, desperately need a tax system under which taxes on
goods to be exported easily can be rebated to help get the
prices down to affordable and competitive levels. That is
difficult to do if a corporate income tax is a prime component of the cost of the goods. Since it is collected on profitability instead of on the basic costs or sales volume, the
corporate income tax cannot be determined in advance,
but only long after the goods have been exported and sold.

This really is one of the more formidable reasons why
American goods so often are unable to compete in foreign
markets. The problem has been recognized for some years
and the Domestic International Sales Corporation (DISC)
law was enacted to try to cope with it. The DISC law gave
large American companies which operate internationally a
chance to offset some of the competitive disadvantages in
foreign trade of the U.S. corporate income tax. But the
DISC program aroused the stupid opposition of populist
politicians and economists who imagined it was only a corporate tax shelter. They shouted dogmatically that American corporations must be taxed on all the profit they
earned anywhere in the world without regard for the economic realities of global price competition.

We need a corporate tax system that will make it much
easier to get the prices of American products down on
world markets if we ever are to restore employment in
American manufacturing to anything like past levels.

But the most serious flaw with a system that taxes business on profitability instead of activity did not become glaringly apparent until the stagflation recession of 1981 and 1982. If you examine the quarterly earnings of major corporations in the first two quarters of 1982 you are at once struck by the fact that a very small decline in sales produced a huge profit shrinkage or even a loss under stagflation conditions, and many companies had sharply lower earnings in spite of higher sales.

This means the government is going to take a huge decline in corporate income tax collections for the period. On the other hand, if the companies were taxed on activity— i.e., sales, value-added, cash flow or other transactional bases—the shrinkage in corporate tax collections would be quite modest and the federal deficit would be significantly less.

The corporate income tax distorts and perverts all American economic policy and corporate management. No manager can make any plan without giving paramount attention to the tax advantages or disadvantages of his decisions. The tax also grossly distorts accounting procedures and makes many profit and loss statements fly directly in the face of common sense. For example, a company has an operating loss of five million dollars but the accountant insists on deducting from this loss a two-million dollar reserve for income taxes that don't have to be paid, thus reducing the loss reported to shareholders to three million dollars. Or under certain circumstances, the tax reserve is added to the operating loss, thus magnifying the loss reported to shareholders.

The reasons given by the accounting profession for doing this and the reasons the Internal Revenue Service gives for allowing it to be done do not add up to common sense. The reasons grow out of a complicated system by which the IRS allows companies that lose money to carry part of the losses forward or backward to offset profits earned in other years, thus compounding and aggravating the evil of rewarding inefficiently run companies and companies that deliberately pile up losses to evade taxes.

The corporate income tax has made a scandalous racket

out of the depreciation of buildings, machinery and other property. Time was when a depreciation schedule was only an honest and sensible way of setting up reserves to replace buildings and equipment as they wore out or became obsolescent. Under the high corporate income tax, accelerated depreciation has become a way of avoiding taxes and inflating both profits and costs to consumers. This is so because depreciation is deductible from taxable income, as it should be. But under an extremely elaborate code of IRS rules and special laws passed by Congress, depreciation has become a field of enormous and devious manipulation by accountants, lawyers, corporate managers and the promoters of a wide variety of tax-sheltered investment schemes.

The worst of these tax-sheltered investment schemes are targeted at evasion or avoidance of the federal individual income tax rather than the corporate tax. In fact some of the tax shelters favored by corporations were authorized by Congress for quite legitimate purposes—for example, to encourage the building of housing or the exploration and drilling for oil and gas.

But lately we have seen a new manifestation: salable depreciation tax shelters. This is done under a law enacted comparatively recently by Congress. A corporation makes an arrangement with a leasing company under which the corporation pays the leasing firm for the use of valuable machinery and retains the tax depreciation rights on the machinery. It then sells these depreciation rights to another company that uses them to offset taxable profits. Hundreds of millions of dollars worth of these lease-deal tax depreciation rights have been sold by companies that did not have big current profits to offset by accelerated depreciation credits. The companies that bought the depreciation rights paid handsome prices for them and it was quite a gamble for some of them; if their business goes sour in the years immediately ahead, they will not have big profits to offset and the money they paid for the depreciation rights could be lost.

The probability is that this whole business of salable tax depreciation rights will cost the government hundreds of millions of dollars in corporate income tax that otherwise would have to be paid. To many persons it looks like a shameless scam. There already is a fairly strong movement on Capitol Hill to put an end to it.

During the affluent 1960s the corporate tax loss carry forward and carry back rules of the IRS were interpreted so liberally that corporations with big losses on their books, even companies that were bankrupt, were in great demand as merger and acquisition targets for profitable companies that could use the losses to offset taxes on their own profits. The rules are more rigorously interpreted nowadays and there aren't so many affluent companies, but this trend could reappear. It is another prime example of the absurdity of taxing corporations on profitability instead of activity.

It can be argued that the corporate income tax is inflationary because it increases the cost of doing business and hence forces prices up. But this is not easy to prove and some economists claim all taxes are inherently anti-inflationary because they sop up excess money supply and help slow down inflationary demand for goods and services. Other experts are equally convinced that high taxes are inflationary because they encourage government extravagance and that government spending is the greatest cause of inflation.

In any case, the evidence is abundant that the only good thing that can be said about the corporate income tax is that it raises revenue for the government; but there are other taxes that can raise revenue faster—the value-added tax or some other form of transactional or consumption tax which taxes activity, not profitability.

The value-added tax, the most frequently proposed alternative to the corporate income tax, is a sort of pyramiding sales tax that is levied at every stage of manufacturing or processing that adds a little to the value of finished products. It is collected as the goods are produced and sold, so manufacturers, distributors and marketers can calculate its impact precisely in advance. It is also very easy to exempt goods to be exported from the value-added tax, so it does not help price goods out of foreign markets as the corporate income tax does.

It is much used in Europe because it raises revenue so rapidly and is so favorable to a nation's export trade.

Agitation in favor of the value-added tax never has made headway in the United States because of the opposition of labor unions, most politicians and some economists who claim it is regressive, that its burden would fall largely on mass consumers rather than on the well-to-do. However, in the final analysis, it also is consumers who pay in higher prices for the corporate income tax. A corporation usually has only three sources of cash flow—sales, capital gains and yield on investments. Of these three categories, sales outweigh capital gains and investment income combined by a large margin. Therefore, it is clear that the government is looking to collect the corporate income tax from the sales dollars provided by consumers. To argue, as is often done, that the corporate income tax comes only out of the pockets of stockholders is a false assumption. So there is good reason to believe that the corporate income tax may be every bit as regressive as a value-added tax would be.

Of course, if a value-added tax or any other consumption tax on corporate receipts were simply imposed in addition to the corporate income tax as has been done in some countries, it then would prove very regressive. If a value-added tax is adopted in the United States, the corporate income tax should be abolished, lock, stock and barrel.

Because an increasing share of the American economy now is devoted to services which do not lend themselves so readily to step-by-step calculation and imposition of a value-added tax, there would have to be some accompanying form of transaction or consumption tax suited to service industries.

One caution. It also would be necessary to find a new way to prevent the excessive hoarding of undistributed profits by closely held corporations in order to evade the individual income tax and pile up new investment income on the retained earnings.

It is not only the corporate income tax that needs to be changed; our whole national tax system should be overhauled to stop the drift of business and labor into the underground economy, to halt manifest injustices that have crept into the structure of the individual income tax over the years and to recapture vast amounts of revenue for the government on income that is escaping taxation through a huge jumble of exclusions, loopholes and shelters.

Also we need tax simplification. The present twelve-step progressive individual income tax is over-complicated and forces people to make out complex returns or pay accountants and lawyers to do it for them.

The system is subject to gross abuses. There are well authenticated cases of extremely wealthy persons, including one billionaire, who paid practically no income tax in many years because they invested mainly in tax-exempt state and municipal bonds and made judicious purchases of participations in enterprises with such liberal tax shelter provisions that the excess tax shelters from loss or depreciation offset their salaries and other taxable income. Inflated deductions for charitable contributions and the creation of personal "foundations" with dubious intentions are other types of abuses.

The structure of the steeply progressive individual income tax also has some serious faults. One is "bracket creep," the increase in tax burden when inflationary salary or other income boosts force the taxpayer into a higher tax bracket and wipes out virtually all the benefit of the income gain. Another structural fault is the marriage penalty: two young persons who both are working discover that after they marry, their combined incomes push them into a higher tax bracket.

Over the years the structure of the income tax also has been distorted as Congress adopted a large number of special tax benefit provisions for corporations and special groups of individual taxpayers, ostensibly in the public interest. An article in the *Wall Street Journal* on July 8, 1982, said there are more than one hundred of these special provisions, which congressmen call "tax expenditures," and that they amounted to about $253 billion a year in income of various types that was escaping taxation. The Senate Budget Committee expressed alarm at the rapid growth of these tax expenditure giveaways and said that at the rate pressure groups were getting them enacted they might reach $440 billion a year by 1987.

Currently there is much agitation for a "flat" income tax

to solve all these problems and raise more revenue for the government by recapturing and taxing the vast sums that now go into the underground economy. The IRS claims it is losing $95 billion a year, almost a quarter as much as it actually collects, in income and Social Security taxes on income diverted to the underground economy. I believe this $95 billion is far too low. Other experts say the IRS is exaggerating this sum but even the most critical of these experts say the amount lost is between $28 billion and $42 billion a year.

President Reagan has declared his sympathy with the idea of a flat income tax, saying its promise is "very tempting" and "worth looking into." He said he did not think abolishing the tax deduction for contributions as part of a flat income tax program would stop people from making gifts to worthy causes.

Conservative economist Milton Friedman of the University of Chicago has been advocating a flat income tax for twenty years. He and other advocates believe the flat tax rate really would cause much of the activity in the underground economy to surface so its revenues could be taxed. Perhaps, this is a highly debatable supposition but the underground economy now poses such a threat to our future that any proposed way to bring it under control deserves consideration.

Another reason advanced in favor of the flat income tax is that it would be much easier to administer and collect than the present steeply progressive tax, and accordingly would slash the IRS payroll substantially.

A pure flat income tax would do away with virtually all deductions, exclusions, tax credits and tax shelters. Social Security benefits, veterans' benefits and interest on state and municipal bonds, which presently are excluded from taxable income, might be fully taxed. Capital gains would be included in ordinary income and would pay the full rate instead of the approximately half rates at which they now are taxed. There would be no more deductions for home mortgage interest or interest on personal loans, or state and local taxes or for charitable, religious and educational gifts or for extraordinary medical expenses. And some but not all of the business expense deductions presently allowed under the individual income tax would disappear.

There still would be personal exemptions and these would be somewhat more liberal than those allowed under the present law.

The rates usually proposed by advocates of a flat income tax range from 12 to 19 percent, and the rate would be imposed on individuals and corporations alike. Individuals would be taxed on every penny of income over and above their personal exemptions, corporations on every cent they take in over and above genuine operating and financing expenses. At least one of the plans also would grant corporations significant "capital recovery" allowances. Most flat rate tax advocates favor abolishing tax credits on losses to be carried forward to offset taxable income in future years.

A pure flat tax, thus, would be such a radical departure from our present system that it would destroy some businesses and force extremely drastic changes in others. It would take a constitutional amendment in all likelihood to tax the interest income from state and municipal bonds. Depriving the states, cities and other local government agencies of the right to issue tax-exempt securities would force them to borrow at the same high interest rates paid by corporations and the federal government and its agencies. This could have a crippling impact on local government and on education.

Similarly, abolishing the tax deduction for interest on home mortgages would deal the already hard-hit housing industry a terrible blow. Conceivably, it might cause the present high-priced home market to collapse with resulting big losses for many families. On the other hand, doing away with the deduction for mortgage interest on family-owned homes might create a huge demand for rental housing and spur speculative building of rental units. After all, interest and other financing charges on housing built as rental units still would be fully tax deductible as an ordinary cost of doing business under the purest type of flat income tax.

The manifest difficulties of a pure flat tax are so great that none of the flat tax plans actually proposed is anything like pure. None of them go so far as to tax Social Security benefits or interest income on state and municipal bonds, and some would even allow deductions for home mortgage interest, state and local taxes and certain contributions. Some of them don't even have a true flat tax, they simply would reduce the present twelve progressive steps to about four or would have a basic flat tax with surtaxes for larger incomes.

The advocates of these various proposals all believe, possibly on substantial grounds, that their programs could balance the federal budget and even produce an annual surplus within three or four years. The big question, of course, is who really would pay for this budget balancing?

The critics of the flat tax philosophy, who include labor leaders, politicians and economists, all insist that the flat tax would increase the tax burden of low-income groups and reduce the payments of the rich. Joseph J. Minarik, an economist for the Congressional Budget Office, recently produced a chart showing that a pure flat tax with a rate of 11.8 percent with no exemptions or deductions would raise the proportion of total income taxes paid by families with incomes of $10,000 to $20,000 a year from 13.8 percent to 19.4 percent, but would cut the tax share of families with incomes exceeding $100,000 a year in half, from 16.1 percent to 8.1 percent. Families in the $20,000 to $30,000 income bracket also would pay more, but those in the $30,000 to $40,000 income group would get some relief from their current tax burden.

Minarik used the actual tax returns and collections for 1981 as his data base, so it is clear he was not envisioning a flat tax that would go so far as to tax Social Security benefits or interest on state and municipal bonds.

Fortune magazine said in its July 26, 1982, issue that Minarik's chart demonstrated that "the trouble with the flat tax is that it punishes the poor."

On the other hand, David Hale, an economist for Kemper Financial Services, told the Heritage Foundation that he believed the chief effect of a flat income tax would be to give middle-income taxpayers the same relief the reduction of the peak rate from 70 to 50 percent gave the rich.

Republican Senator Mark Hatfield of Oregon says he favors the flat tax as a way to get the government out of the business of using the tax code for social engineering. Hatfield says, "By attempting to solve every social and economic problem through the tax code, we have put a greater and greater burden on the taxpayer."

For a different view of the flat tax, let us take a look at the proposal of Professors Robert E. Hall and Alvin Rabushka, both senior fellows of the Hoover Institution at Stanford University in California. They claim that adoption of a simply 19 percent flat income tax automatically would balance the federal budget within three years if Congress continues to support the Reagan economy program.

Hall and Rabushka originally advanced their ideas in an article in the *Wall Street Journal* in December, 1981. They claimed adoption of their plan ultimately would bring the prevailing high interest rates down by greatly reducing the Treasury's borrowing needs and that the low flat rate income tax would draw economic activity from the underground economy into the legitimate taxed economy, and this eventually could make it possible to slash the flat tax rate from 19 to 17 or even 16 percent.

The notion that lower tax rates will cause people to desert the underground economy may be true. After all, although workers who get paid "under the table" evade taxes, they also miss out on the best investment bargain currently available, Social Security. Nevertheless, it sounds a little like suggesting that a thief who would steal twenty-five dollars a week would turn honest rather than steal ten dollars a week.

Hall and Rabushka are on much more solid ground when they note that "those nations with lower marginal tax rates have achieved [the most] economic growth over the past decade." They also are right when they say that the United States in the post-war era has had its periods of most vigorous economic growth and reduced inflation following cuts in marginal tax rates. They add that "a simplified tax with low marginal rates would help restore confidence in government and would support the basic honesty of the American people."

The Hall-Rabushka program would allow personal exemptions of $6,200 for a married couple, $3,800 for a single person, $5,600 for a single head of household and $750 for each additional dependent, but there would be absolutely no deductions. However, the figures they quote from their data base indicate that Hall and Rabushka also do not contemplate taxing Social Security benefits or interest on state and municipal bonds.

Hall and Rabushka claim that the flat tax and the enlarged personal exemptions would be progressive in their real impact. They say a family with income of $10,000 a year would pay only 4.4 percent of family income in taxes, a family with income of $15,000 would pay 9.2 percent, a family with $30,000 income 14.1 percent; a $40,000 a year household would pay 15.2 percent and a $50,000 income family 16.1 percent.

The Achilles heel of the Hall-Rabushka plan may lie in its application to corporations. Hall and Rabushka say that if their flat tax had been in effect in 1981, individual income taxpayers would have paid $213 billion that year instead of the $289 billion actually collected, but that the 19 percent flat tax they recommend would have raised $133 billion from corporations instead of the $57 billion actually collected.

But that still would be taxing business on profitability instead of activity, and in a bad business year, such as 1982, it could lead to a huge shortfall in revenue and a big government deficit.

Hall and Rabushka say the net revenues of U.S. business in 1981 were $1,050 billion after what they consider proper expenses. Their plan would give business capital recovery allowances against these net revenues that would have amounted to $349 billion in 1981, leaving $701 billion as taxable income. The $57 billion in taxes collected under the 1981 corporate income tax would amount to only 8.1 percent of what Hall and Rabushka consider to be true taxable corporate income, even though the peak corporate tax rate was 46 percent.

The Hall-Rabushka plan also has an indexing feature that would increase the personal exemptions under the flat 19 percent individual income tax for offsetting inflation.

Advocates of the flat tax also have to deal with the obvious fact that the present tax system is so interwoven with many of our social and economic institutions that it would be next to impossible to junk the present system altogether. There are too many influential people who depend on the present exclusions, deductions and shelters for their livings to make adoption of anything resembling a pure flat tax politically possible, and even a modified flat tax plan could hardly pass unless it was accompanied by a very big tax cut, and, in the present level of inflation and big spending on defense, another big federal tax slash hardly seems in the cards.

Nevertheless, as Mr. Reagan says, the flat tax is well worth looking into because, at the very least, under a flat tax everybody would be able to keep busy earning more money without the fear that his or her efforts would be punished by having to pay ever higher taxes.

But if a flat tax were enacted that did not tax interest on presently exempt state and municipal securities or do away with most tax shelters and tax expenditure benefits, it would not solve the problem of those few very rich individuals who currently pay virtually no income tax. Obviously, this is not a gigantic economic problem but, morally, it infuriates people to learn that a Texas billionaire paid practically no income tax for several years running.

But individuals and corporations keep looking avidly for tax shelters. They get into them, often paying handsomely for the privilege, both to get participation in losses or depreciation reserves to be used as write-offs to offset their other taxable income; and, as in the case of many tax-sheltered real estate and oil and gas drilling syndications, there is a chance for a big long-term profit.

The tax shelters are based on depreciation and what are known as the "intangible costs" in oil and gas drilling—the risk of dry holes, for example. One thing about legitimate tax shelters that most people do not realize is that they don't last, they only defer and do not permanently eliminate tax liability if profits eventually accrue. The depreciation schedules run out and the reserves for intangible drilling costs decline. The purchased participation eventually will become a tax liability instead of a shelter.

So, the wealthy tax-shelter addict keeps selling out of older syndications as they near the cross-over point to profitability and buying new ones that still have big current losses or depreciation reserves. That is where the promoters of tax shelters and the brokers who sell them on fat commissions come in. An article by Deborah Rankin in *The New York Times* on August 8, 1982, quotes Robert A. Stanger & Co. of Fair Haven, New Jersey, which publishes authoritative books and periodicals on tax shelters, as saying $8 billion worth of participations in tax shelters were sold in the United States in 1981. Stanger said half of this money went into oil and gas drilling, 32 percent into real estate shelters and the rest was divided up among equipment leasing, cattle herd leasing, cattle feeding and cable television ventures for the most part. In the privately offered participations, the minimum investment required usually is $50,000 to $150,000; in those offered to the public, the minimum may be only $5,000.

Only in a few privately financed real estate shelters is it possible for the taxpayer to legitimately get a write-off exceeding his original investment, and he usually will recover that and some profit in addition. There are lots of advertisements in various publications and in the mails offering tax shelters of three and four times the initial investment, but all of these are of dubious legality and many of them are outright frauds. The taxpayer who buys them and attempts to use the write-offs to offset his other income may end up in most serious trouble with Uncle Sam.

The Stanger Company's figure of $8 billion for the amount of tax-shelter promotions sold in the United States in 1981 appears to cover only the legitimate deals. The volume for the illegal shelter promotions sold is not known but undoubtedly is much smaller. People keep buying the dubious shelters either out of ignorance or because they are born gamblers and just take a chance on their tax returns not being audited so the illegal tax-shelter write-off won't be detected. But tax-shelter experts say the odds now are much in favor of the phony shelter being caught by the IRS.

It is unlikely that any flat tax plan that tolerated tax shelters on the scale they are presently being used would achieve the benefits its advocates hope for. The Hall-Rabushka plan and the other flat tax programs presently being pushed actively would not interfere greatly with existing tax shelters unless Congress changed the formula for defining adjusted income. Under the present law business losses, which include tax-shelter write-offs, come off total income to create adjusted income from which deductions and personal exemptions are subtracted to establish taxable income on the individual return. If a flat income tax law continued this practice, tax shelters would not be affected by the abolition of deductions. So, unless the lower rates of the flat tax simply made rich taxpayers feel much less in need of shelters, a flat tax law might have little impact on their popularity and use.

One thing is certain, though: taxing corporations on activity through a value-added tax or some other kind of transactional or consumption tax instead of by an income tax would end corporations' need for the present shelters. No income tax, no shelters.

But the public and the government undoubtedly would wish to continue to provide a variety of financial incentives to various business activities—building homes, drilling for oil and gas and other minerals, investment in new plants and machinery in many industries, recycling waste products, for example. This is done generally now by tax credits and special deductions on corporate income. So, if the corporate income tax were abolished, Congress would have to find new kinds of incentives, perhaps credits or refunds against new taxes on corporate activity, or perhaps tax incentives would be replaced altogether by government loans at very low subsidized interest rates. The government would have to borrow the money for such loans in the open market at higher rates and the difference between the rates it paid and the rates it got in return would be the actual amount of the subsidies borne by the taxpayers. The loans would be for specified purposes. The federal government already is doing this on a fairly substantial scale to help a variety of small businesses. The government also makes loans through the Export Import Bank to help American exports.

The individual income tax is as much based on profitability as the corporate income tax is under the present system. If a farmer or the proprietor of an unincorporated business has a loss big enough to offset his salary and other personal income after personal exemptions and allowable deductions, he pays no income tax for that year.

The tax law, in effect, seeks to determine how much of an individual taxpayer's total personal income, minus business losses, is taxable profit. It makes reasonably good sense for the government to tax individual income on this basis, but we already have seen that taxing corporations on the basis of profitability leads to monstrous absurdities and distortions of the entire economy.

It should be emphasized again that this whole idea of taxing business on the basis of profitability began with the first levying of the income tax in 1913, so it is a relatively new idea in our national history. We are left with the sober conclusion that we have become far too dependent on this tax on profit, and this over-dependence on the income tax distorts our whole economy, erodes business activity and definitely has a corrupting influence on American society.

Flattening out the income tax rates, eliminating many of its complexities and simplifying its structure and procedures might help substantially, but the truth is that our entire national and local tax structure needs drastic overhaul and reform.

Many parts of the system are subject to easy abuse or are even dubious in their theoretical base. For example, the liquor and tobacco industries have insisted for many years that the taxes on their products are too high and that they encourage moonshine distilling, cigarette bootlegging and tax stamp counterfeiting. Congress never has been willing to test the theory that lower taxes would raise just as much revenue because they would make these illegal activities less profitable and discourage them. Obviously lower taxes would be socially desirable if they raised the same amount of revenue.

The Social Security and other federal and state payroll taxes on business, which add up to 14 percent or more of payroll in some states, are subject to various abuses. One of the most glaring arises from the fact that, on the portion of the tax that goes to finance unemployment benefits, the rate charged the individual employer varies according to the number of claims filed by persons leaving his employment. Persons who quit jobs of their own accord or who are fired for sufficient cause, insubordination or dishonesty, for example, are not supposed to be eligible for jobless benefits. Yet the people who administer the claims frequently take the word of the applicant that he or she has been laid off or terminated without sufficient cause even though the employer objects strenuously and says the claimant is not entitled to benefits. The claim is granted. This not only costs the taxpayers money unlawfully, it runs up the tax bill of the employer unjustly.

The electronic computer has greatly helped the federal government and the states and municipalities in enforcing the tax laws; you can't quarrel with the computer's arithmetic and it does at lightning speed work that used to require armies of clerks. But all our tax systems still are run by people and are subject at times to political favoritism, bureaucratic incompetence, arrogance and vindictiveness. Several former IRS officials have written fascinating books and articles about the inside workings of the service that reveal this. Human nature being what it is, big corporations and very wealthy individuals with their bold, clever lawyers and accountants are able to wear down the IRS officials and win scandalous bargains in settling big tax disputes, while the IRS agents often adopt an aggressive, bullying tone and tactics in order to win easy victories by riding roughshod over little taxpayers who have aroused their ire.

By and large, though, the IRS has been rather remarkably apolitical most of the time and efficient and clean over the years as compared with other government agencies.

The worst tax scandals in America are local and always have been. People with some political "in" get away with ridiculously low tax assessments on their property and with brazen and defiant evasion of taxes for years running.

Equally scandalous is the way in which state, local and even federal taxes are raised by politicians in plain repudiation and defiance of their campaign pledges to cut taxes.

That is what makes possible so much local and national government extravagance. Seventy years ago in many parts of the country all tax boosts had to be submitted to the voters for ratification. That is no longer the case; perhaps it should be tried again.

President Reagan has endorsed the proposed amendment requiring a balanced federal budget. That should curb the spending powers of Congress if the amendment is ever ratified. But it also could give Congress and federal bureaucrats a new excuse for raising taxes unconscionably. "The Constitution now requires us to raise taxes to pay for the things the people say they want," the pious humbugs on Capitol Hill would be able to say.

We need to broaden the tax base, and we need to greatly reduce dependence on the income tax and put more emphasis on transactional and consumption taxes that are not dependent on profitability and are not so vulnerable to the vicissitudes of clever manipulation, chicanery or plain bad management in business. Such transactional and consumption taxes raise revenue more rapidly; they are difficult to evade but are easy to rebate on goods to be exported. Most importantly, they do not put tremendously prejudicial pressures on managerial and investment decisions.

And, of course, we need tax reforms that discourage government extravagance, both at the national and local levels.

Just taxation is the oldest economic problem of society anywhere in the world. It never has been solved to anywhere near complete satisfaction and probably never will be. The American tax system was for many years the best in the world. Today, most American economists and businessmen would say it is a creaking and oppressive anachronism.

The worst single cause of our high tax burden is the rise in the last half of this century of a huge army of professional politicians. They not only draw large salaries and pensions, either from elective or bureaucratic posts, they also initiate enormously extravagant activities in order to appeal to self-serving voters. And the nation abounds in self-serving voters, all eager to pressure the politicians to favor their particular schemes for feeding at the public trough.

The founding fathers of the republic did not foresee this. They lived in a largely agrarian society of farmers and tradesmen, all independent except for the black slaves. They expected members of the Congress and the state legislatures and all public officials, including the governors of the states, the president and his cabinet and even judges, to be temporary public servants, not professionals. The idea of a pension for anyone except lifelong members of the armed forces would have seemed unwise to George Washington, Thomas Jefferson, Andrew Jackson or even to Abraham Lincoln. Even in the first half of this century, the number of real professionals in American politics was small. Hardly anyone expected to make a living out of holding elective office, much less of having a fat expense account or ever enjoying a large government pension.

The creation in the nineteenth century of the Civil Service put an end ultimately to the "spoils system" of handing out government jobs, but it did not, as was hoped, put an end to the appointment of greedy, incompetent and unscrupulous party hangers-on to all kinds of government jobs, even the most important. It merely made it difficult or impossible to get rid of these extravagant and unsavoury characters once they got on the public payroll, and it gave them the chance to organize and set in motion the machinery for looting the federal and state treasures on a gargantuan scale.

The point is that the government jobholders were, for the most part, temporary appointees until about the mid-1930s, and they lacked the power to impose their will on the people and bring about the squandering of tax money we see today.

So, the creation of the Civil Service may well have bred evils every bit as serious as those it cured.

The rise of the professional politician who spends his or her entire working life holding or seeking elective office or the higher appointive offices has been even more expensive for the American taxpayer. It has made it nearly impossible for a private citizen of great ability and high character to hope for election to office or to exercise the slightest influence on public affairs because the professional politicians now constitute a tacitly organized, privileged, arrogant and avaricious class, like the bureaucrats, with the collective power to control the selection of candidates.

Professionalism has prevailed in American politics now for half a century and it has produced no evidence that it provides anything of value to the public or the cause of good government. The typical professional politician is good at only one thing, getting elected, and to that end he or she sacrifices everything: truth, honor, and personal, political and fiscal responsibility. Greed and ambition are the professional politician's only readily discernible qualities.

Perhaps we should try to get part of the way back to what the founding fathers had in mind. Maybe we should outlaw the profession of politics by limiting tenure in all public offices, elected and appointive, to a single term and abolishing all government pensions except for the uniformed forces and credentialed scientists and technicians, including the judiciary.

That would chop many billions of dollars off the taxpayers' burden.

Of course, it is politically impossible to go far or fast in this direction, but a start could be made by limiting the tenure of senators and members of the House of Representatives and depriving them of the hope of pensions. Once these elected legislators were brought to heel and again put under the control of the voters, the bureaucrats would have lost their strongest allies and in turn ultimately could be brought under effective control of the voters.

We always have had some professionals in American politics and a few of them have been vigorous, responsible and imaginative men—Abraham Lincoln, the two Roosevelts, Harry Truman, Alfred E. Smith and Fiorello LaGuardia, for example. But the run-of-the-mill professional politician is from a much inferior mold, he is not responsible or imaginative although he may be vigorous, and he surrenders readily to any wasteful and extravagant expediency if he thinks it will win him votes.

The Victorian English, who accomplished much in the world, distrusted professionalism in politics and many other fields. They didn't believe any man could be wholly responsible in an objective way about any activity on which his livelihood depended; they thought the professional never could be trusted to put the interest of his clients or the general welfare ahead of his selfish personal goals.

Of course, to define professionalism entirely in terms of devoting one's whole time to something for pay may be a narrow way of looking at it. Many persons think of professionalism as a matter of devotion to a set of standards, but that is the last concern of the typical professional politician.

In spite of the great political acumen he has displayed in getting elected to office and getting his programs enacted, Ronald Reagan is not a professional politician. He has devoted the greater part of his life to the entertainment business and was very successful at it, both as an actor and a film personality. He never has been dependent on politics for a livelihood.

VII

The Moles

BIG GOVERNMENT and professionalism in politics and bureaucracy have a lot more to answer for than high taxes. In the considered opinion of most careful observers, they are responsible for the disastrous growth in the past decade of the underground economy.

In the United States the underground economy, at least inasmuch as we distinguish it from the ordinary criminal economy, is a relatively new phenomenon, but in the world as a whole it is as old as taxation. Some people always have tried and succeeded in evading lawful taxation on activities that are not unlawful in themselves; only the tax evasion is illegal and immoral. Of course, if we consider the total subterranean economy to include all gainful activity that manages to escape taxation, then we must include ordinary crime such as burglary, robbery, forgery, racketeering, narcotic trafficking, smuggling, counterfeiting and so on. The writers of recent books on the subject generally do include ordinary crime in the underground economy.

However, although we have had ordinary crime to deal with in the United States since the earliest days of the Union, large-scale tax evasion by otherwise law-abiding persons did not start until about twenty-five years ago after the

rise in big government had become pronounced and oppressive and our corps of elected and appointed public officials had become completely professionalized. Italy,
France and some other European countries and all Asian
lands had suffered from the deadly effects of the underground economy for at least a century before we Americans began to feel its first blighting touch.

Today every country in the world, including the communist lands, has a subterranean economy, but here in America we have one of the biggest. Nobody knows how big it is.
Estimates range from $200 billion to $700 billion a year,
and from 8 percent to 30 percent of the legitimate taxed
economy in size. This inability to measure the underground economy with any accuracy is one of its most deadly effects. We know it is big enough so that its existence
distorts all the government statistics that measure the regular economy; it means our Gross National Product is
greater than the government says it is, for example, but we
don't know how much greater. We know that the vast number of persons working in the untaxed and undertaxed underground economy, the people who are paid "under the
table" in cash, means unemployment is not as large as the
government figures claim, but we don't know how much
less it is.

We know that a lot of persons who are drawing public
welfare payments are working and are being paid illegally,
but we don't know how many. We know that the growth of
the underground economy has eroded public morality and
civic responsibility in a large part of a whole generation of
Americans, but we are not sure just how widespread this is.
The most terrible thing is that we have very little idea how
to go about correcting this frightful situation, how to collect
the tax revenues the government needs, how to restore
faith and confidence in the government and personal civic
responsibility in our country.

We have one very definite idea of what to do about it. If
it is true, as most experts who have studied the matter believe, that big government, excessively high taxes and self-
centered professionalism in politics and government service are responsible for the growth of the subterranean

economy, then all three of these evils must be mitigated substantially. It would be good to eliminate them, but how to go about even mitigating them is the $64,000 question nobody can even start to answer as yet.

Another thing we know about the underground economy is that the professional politicians and bureaucrats and even the economists keep trying to pretend it doesn't exist or to minimize estimates of its size in plain contradiction of the observable facts. They take this ostrich-like, head-in-the-sand attitude because, once they admit the existence of a huge underground economy, they are forced also to admit that virtually all the statistical data that they grind out and publish at such expense and that forms the basis on which they formulate their observations and conclusions and promulgate policy, rules and regulations are false. The existence of the underground economy makes clowns out of all politicians and bureaucrats and even some of our most influential economists.

Dan Bawly, author of about the most comprehensive and incisive book in the field,* says that most modern economists are "only two-dimensional technicians" anyway, "without plan or program or a serious evaluation of what the optimal, most effective tax structure for the long term should be. There are no social scientists in office who can conceive a policy as radical, say, as how to halve the government budget." In other words, most economists, like most politicians and officials, are mere paper dolls and we can hope for very little from them.

But if we can't quantify the underground economy accurately, at least we do have some descriptions of it and of the way it is changing society. Bawly's book contains scores of references to books and articles on the subject around the world and in great depth. Bawly is an Israeli and a top partner in the American-based international accounting firm, Horwath & Horwath.

Professor Peter M. Gutman of Baruch College of the City University of New York was the first American economist

*The Subterranean Economy, by Dan Bawly, McGraw-Hill, New York, 1982.

to try to measure the underground economy of the United States. In 1977, he calculated that for the year 1976 the underground economy was 10 percent as big as the legitimate taxed economy. He reached this conclusion by an analytical comparison of the amount of money in circulation with income tax collections. Bawly calls Gutman's estimate too conservative and Gutman admitted in the fall of 1981 that this probably is true. The Internal Revenue Service ultimately was goaded into its own estimate of the scope of underground economy, which turned out to be 9 percent as big as the regular economy.

In an article in *The New Jersey Bell Journal* in the fall of 1981, Gutman cited four other estimates. Charles Haulk of the Federal Reserve Bank of Atlanta put the size of the underground economy at 16 percent of the regular economy, Professor Edward Feige of the University of Wisconsin put it at 30 percent and two other estimates put it at 8 percent.

In dollars, Gutman calculated the volume of the underground economy for calendar 1981 at $310 billion, but said it could have been $420 billion.

A later study by the Louis Harris public opinion polling organization for *Business Week* magazine's October 11, 1982, edition estimated that moonlighting alone may account for $200 billion a year in underground income. The Harris poll was based on a rather small sample and *Business Week's* editors warned that it should be taken with two grains of salt. Nevertheless, the Harris organization said even the small sample enabled it to reach some definite conclusions. Among these conclusions were:

—That the U.S. underground economy may amount to upwards of $400 billion a year.
—That the underground economy is not a "blue collar" phenomenon. The poll implied that 30 percent of all American families are in some way involved in the underground economy. White families are more likely to be so involved than black families, and more white collar families have someone moonlighting than blue collar families.

—Perhaps the most disturbing thing about the Harris study was that it indicated that the better off Americans are, the more likely they are to have extra earnings that they do not report on their income tax returns as they are supposed to. The worst cheaters were found to be persons in the $35,000 to $50,000 a year income bracket. About 41 percent in this group admitted having income not reported for taxes.

The underground economy is largely, in fact nearly entirely, a matter of cash. Gutman names retailing, service industries, restaurants, construction contractors, home improvement businesses, parking lots, trucking, street vending and several other industries that operate mainly as small businesses as typical of those that insist on cash transactions, keep minimal records and don't pay taxes. He said skimming cash off the top is the favorite way of cheating—collecting sales taxes from customers but not remitting it to the city or state, for example. Another is to hire people for cash to work "off the books"; the employer saves Social Security and workingman's compensation charges and other costs. The workers evade both income and Social Security taxes.

Proprietors of these all-cash businesses often understate their volume to save on income and other taxes and to cover up the skimming of money "off the top." Some businessmen in the underground economy insist on all-cash transactions in order to be non-existent both to the tax collector and to the other public officials who might become curious about many of their activities—the regulatory authorities dealing with labor, safety and health regulations, for example.

When expense accounts are paid for in cash instead of by check, Gutman says, a lot of cash skimming goes on even in large businesses, and this puts these firms partly in the underground economy.

Like the Harris poll, Gutman says moonlighting is perhaps the biggest single component of the subterranean economy. Both Gutman and Bawly say the number of persons in the United States who moonlight or who simply don't file a return in order to avoid reporting at least a part of their income has grown enormously in the past decade because many people suspect that the IRS is too under-manned to catch them even with the aid of the most sophisticated computers.

On the basis of varied evidence, Gutman calculated that 25 percent of the U.S. labor force, or about 27,000,000 persons, were part of the underground economy in one way or another in 1981.

(With regard to the 10.04 percent unemployment rate as of the end of October, 1982, leaving some 11,000,000 people out of work in the United States, I believe it is necessary to analyze this figure. I really wonder how many of those unemployed, receiving unemployment insurance, might be obtaining income through jobs or businesses in the underground economy. What percentage there is we will never know, because there are certainly no statistics kept on the underground economy. I think the next question is how many of these millions of people are unqualified for any type of job being offered? And that's where our politicians of the past 35 to 40 years have really fallen down on the job. That is where people have lost their self-respect by not having the ability to earn a living because they were not properly trained and educated for adequate employment.)

(Realistically, therefore, we really don't know how many of the 11,000,000 are truly unemployed in this unnatural war going on in the United States economy.)

Gutman also concluded that only one-quarter to one-third of the revenues of the underground economy came from ordinary crime; all the rest was income on which taxes were evaded. Certainly, not all criminal profits go untaxed. Criminals have to pay gasoline and other transaction taxes like the rest of us, and most criminals know that it is much easier as a rule to get caught evading taxes (and be sent to prison) than to get caught in ordinary criminal activities; therefore they often file income tax returns even if they only report a minimal plausible income.

Much of the profit earned in the underground economy naturally is invested in collectibles such as paintings, antiques, Persian rugs and in tax-exempt municipal and state bonds, assets not regularly checked by the IRS.

Gutman reached the following ultimate conclusions:

—The existence of the underground economy means that the U.S. Gross National Product is about 14 percent higher than government figures indicate.

—The population of the United States is greater than official figures indicate because undocumented persons who participate in the underground economy resist being counted in the census.

—Living standards and economic growth are both higher than the government figures show.

—Productivity per worker and per man-hour also is somewhat higher than government statistics indicate. So are savings and investments.

—Poverty in the United States is not as widespread as official figures indicate. Gutman believes that in 1981, fewer than 4 percent of the people were living in poverty in contrast with the 12 percent indicated by government figures.

Of course, Gutman could not prove his numerical estimates of the difference between reality and official statistics. But he felt he had proved that we make great mistakes in government and business policy because of misleading and distorted statistical information created by the existence of the underground economy. The situation perverts the allocation of economic resources and erodes the voluntary foundation of our tax system.

Gutman considers reducing the tax burden and ending inflation to be the only sure way to halt the pernicious growth of the underground economy.

Bawly's picture of the subterranean economy is much more vivid and radical than Gutman's. Where Gutman sees the picture peopled largely by workers and small businessmen, Bawly finds that, in the United States and even more so in continental Europe, individuals of the wealthier classes and middle-sized and big businesses are in the subterranean economy up to their necks. His book is filled with descriptions of tax dodges and tax shelters for the well-to-do that are practiced so widely that, in countries like Italy and France, any attempt to describe the true economy in statistical terms is utterly meaningless, and he implies that this soon could become the case in the United States.

Bawly says bluntly over and over that it is big government that has caused the underground economy in virtually all countries to grow much faster in recent years than the legitimate economy. He says "big brother government," whether in the democracies or under authoritarian dictatorships, has "inevitably led to hardening of the official arteries, to bureaucratic intransigence and inflexibility." The end result, he concludes, is that big government finally comes to exist for no other reason than to perpetuate its structure and the jobs of the bureaucrats and politicians. The interests of the public and the public welfare are not even thought about except in relation to getting votes and collecting taxes. Nobody is the least bit interested in efficient, scientific administration or common sense.

The rapid growth of the underground economy is, thus, the inevitable process of revolt by a large part of the population against big government's incompetence, stagnation and high taxes. Nevertheless, Bawly refuses to regard those who live and work underground as revolutionary pioneers or idealists. "If asked what they are doing or why, they might say they are fighting for survival," he says, "but many may be simply anarchists or just greedy. In many countries, they are the new silent majority, in others a large silent minority."

Bawly not only thinks Gutman's estimate of the size of the U.S. underground economy is too low, he says flatly it is not possible to measure it.

Bawly considers it most significant that the public in most countries no longer attaches any stigma to tax evasion, no matter how flagrant it is. He also claims that this cannot be cured by harsh measures or simply by increasing the number of tax inspectors, creating armies of informers and decreeing more severe penalties. He believes the communist countries suffer more from tax evasion than the western countries, although they have far more inspectors and collectors.

One of the more radical ideas advanced by Bawly is that Big Brother government and the underground economy as a revolt against it both result in substantial degree from perversion of the original concept of the income tax. He says, "Income tax was originally designed to tax the well-to-do, and that at a moderate rate. It was never meant to raise taxes from the general public. Many of its ills result from the fact that in the past generation it has been applied wrongly." He goes on to say, "The blindness of the legislatures throughout the democracies has been and still is that they believe they can turn all the wage and capital earning population into full taxpayers. At no point in history, could this be done."

Also . . . "It is not yet accepted by government that it is impossible to maintain a totally fair, dynamic and equitable tax law at the prevailing welfare state tax rates that will apply to the whole population. . . . The masses who opt for the subterranean economy and choose its path . . . will not willingly agree to pay any tax. They never did, but until World War II, the vast majority of the working population of the United States was not liable for income tax. The highest tax rates then usually were lower than the present *average* minimum of 25 percent."

So, Bawly says, the income levy is totally unsuitable for a broad-based tax, too dependent on voluntary compliance and too complicated and hard to enforce, and he is implying that the development of a vast underground economy with a corrosive and destructive impact on society is the inevitable result of trying to apply the income tax too broadly. The obvious inference is that, just as the corporate income tax penalizes well-run companies and rewards inefficient companies, so a broad-based personal income tax penalizes people for being thrifty and industrious, and they rebel against that. We can go on and infer that transactional and other taxes on activity rather than on personal profitability must be resorted to in order to cure the cancer of the underground economy. Of course, such taxes also can be evaded and are, but on the whole they are somewhat easier to enforce. The income tax could then be restored to its original role of a surtax on very high personal income. Bawly stops short of drawing this inference, however.

Both Gutman and Bawly praised President Reagan's 1981 expense cutting and tax slashing programs as steps in the right direction.

In the non-criminal areas, moonlighting workers, especially women, individuals and businesses who engage in barter on a big scale, and businessmen with virtually unlimited expense accounts, have to be considered the major participants in the underground economy. It is impossible to estimate how much these activities cost the nation in unpaid income taxes.

Throughout history, farmers in all countries have been notable tax resisters and always have been a major part of the underground economy. In former times, their tax resistance was punished savagely to set an example. The Egyptian Pharaohs sold peasants and their wives and children into slavery or even fed them to the crocodiles of the Nile for failure to pay taxes. In the Middle Ages, European peasants sometimes were flogged and hanged for tax evasion. But usually the stubborn resistance of the farmers to taxes won out over the authorities because the peasants could cause famine if pressed too hard.

Bawly says that in the modern world, both in Europe and the United States, farmers generally are taxed at much lower effective rates than the rest of the population and, in effect, operate as part of the subterranean economy because they conduct much of their business on a barter basis and keep few records which the tax collectors can get their hands on.

"There are more opportunities to underreport farm income than other forms of income," he concludes. He goes on to say that while "in most businesses, the purchase of a fixed asset is capitalized and then written off over its expected lifetime, cash accounting allows farmers to write off machinery and other farm equipment in the year of acquisition. Similarly, they may write off the cost of developing or improving their orchards, groves and vineyards."

All this may be technically true, but, although I am a city dweller myself, I fear that Bawly is in this instance suc-

cumbing to the bias of the accountant. He shows little appreciation of how hazardous an occupation farming is ev-
erywhere both financially and otherwise. No other business is subject to such savage price fluctuations, over
which the farmers have no control, or to the devastating
vicissitudes of weather and climate, transport disruptions,
the ravages of insects and plant diseases, and even to soil
pollution and erosion. Even with the most modern machinery, farming still is an arduous and physically dangerous
vocation. No one else in our society is so exposed to sick-
ness and accidents that can be fatal or cripple one for life.

Nevertheless, it probably is true that many farmers operate in a way as to suggest that they are part of the underground economy.

Speculators in gold and silver, jewelry, art objects, antiq-
uities and many other kinds of transactions in which volume can be rather easily understated for bookkeeping purposes, and hence for taxation, comprise another big and
growing segment of the underground economy.

Bawly devotes several chapters to detailing his belief
that multinational corporations and other business firms
engaged in international operations evade billions of dollars in taxes annually or avoid them by means that are bare-
ly legal or of dubious legality, and that they get by with this
only because government revenue services lack the manpower and expertise to check adequately on their activities
and curb the abuses. He thus appears to believe that a
large part of the free enterprise world's legitimate, establishment business firms are in fact living partly in the underground economy and by so doing are contributing to
the destruction of the economies and moral foundations of
western society.

Bawly is a skeptical man, even about his own profession.
He says little can be hoped for from accountants: "In an
age when bureaucratic policies are muddled and incoher-
ent and it is common to admire successful tax avoidance
schemes, members of the accounting profession compete
to provide ideas of how to pay less taxes since those who
do so will earn the most."

Offshore banks in such places as Switzerland, the isle of

Jersey, the Bahamas, the Cayman Islands, Luxembourg, Hong Kong and even London are facilities which enable tens of thousands of rich persons, including speculators and criminals, to hide and "launder" billions of dollars worth of profits earned in the subterranean economy every year and evade taxation on the profits.

The mechanics of how these dubious and frequently blatantly illegal financial manipulations are executed are too intricate to be described here. Even Bawly's account of how it's done is not clear to the layman or the ordinary businessman, but there can be no doubt that his conclusions are in the main right.

In the United States, the evasion of Social Security taxes by persons in the subterranean economy is a most serious matter. In September, 1979, Donald Lubick, an assistant secretary of the Treasury, told a Senate subcommittee that of 50,000 independent construction contractors checked by the IRS, fully half had not reported any income for tax purposes and 60 percent had not paid any Social Security tax. It is certain that the IRS could not have checked anywhere near all the independent building contractors in the country, and if 60 percent of this large sample of just one industry was operating in the underground economy and not paying Social Security taxes themselves or collecting the workers' share of the payroll taxes from their employees and remitting it to the government, then Professor Gutman may be right in guessing that 27,000,000 American workers are not contributing or at least are not contributing adequately to Social Security funds or to income tax funds.

The great problem with our Social Security system is known to be that there are not enough younger workers contributing to the fund to pay the increasing total of benefits being collected by the elderly and disabled. If Gutman is right, it may be that the existence of the underground economy is the chief cause of the Social Security system's problems.

The great question, of course, is just how has big government caused the cancerous growth of the underground economy?

One explanation was given in a speech by Chairman Joseph J. Pinola of Western Bancorporation in San Francisco in 1979. Pinola said the United States had changed from a nation that encouraged productivity into a country in which productivity is penalized. He said inflationary paper profits were unfairly taxed and that this and over-regulation of business had led to a lack of investment and a disenchantment on the part of Americans with saving, a disenchantment so great that, at 4.5 percent a year, our national rate of personal savings now is the lowest in the industrialized world. The fact that inflation has steadily increased everyone's tax liability aggravates the conditions Pinola complained of.

The subterranean economy also includes a gray area of business offenses, activities that are unethical, clearly immoral and often illegal but are not usually associated in the public mind with professional or organized criminals. These offenses are carried out by supposedly respectable businessmen and their employees. They siphon off billions of dollars from business every year and very little of this hidden or stolen money is ever reported on tax returns, for obvious reasons.

The offenses include bankruptcy-related frauds, bribery, kickbacks and payoffs, computer crimes, insurance frauds, credit card and bad check swindles, receiving stolen property, undervaluing inventories and physical property for taxation, conspiracy to commit arson, fraudulent charity and donation rackets, and even the setting up of phony religious foundations to evade taxes.

Proportionately, the largest subterranean economy in the western world is in Italy. The greater part of Italy's economy has gone underground. We Americans tend to think of Italy as an impoverished, run-down country, virtually reduced to anarchy by a corrupt, hopelessly inefficient government and bureaucracy in which the elementary administration of justice and virtually all public services have deteriorated to utter undependability.

But Americans who go to Italy and stay long enough to see beneath the surface say the country is far from impoverished, that it is prosperous and vigorous and its economy is growing—but it is all invisible insofar as official figures are concerned. The average Italian family may well be earning four times as much as the government says it is. Italy is the best customer in the world, after the United States, for Rolls-Royce automobiles, Scotch whiskey, French champagne and other luxuries.

But Italy really is living in a state of virtual anarchy. The government's authority is gravely compromised and government services are so poor you can't even mail a letter and count on it to be delivered. The average Italian appears to think anyone is an idiot to pay full taxes in a country where the government gives one so little back in return for his money.

Whether bad government in Italy drove the economy underground or the subterranean economy wrecked the government may be another version of the chicken and egg conundrum, but the point is that the same thing could happen in the United States if we don't bring our underground economy under control.

And no matter how prosperous an underground economy becomes, it still is a society in which there can be no long-term safety or protection for anyone. Businessmen in an underground economy often cannot hope to buy insurance against fires, floods, thefts and other disasters. Either they dare not apply for fear of drawing attention to their corrupt practices, or the insurance companies simply will not cover them. Workers in the subterranean economy can't get medical insurance, Social Security or even union protection. They are driven often to allying themselves with gang bosses. And neither the employers nor the workers can get protection against extortion and bribery demands. They can't go to the courts and sue for damages when they have just grievances without exposing themselves to prosecution.

VIII

The Fifth Horseman

IF SAINT JOHN THE DIVINE had been of a little more worldly turn of mind he undoubtedly would have listed five horsemen instead of the four apocalyptical knights of disaster in the Book of Revelation.

To war, famine, pestilence and death he would have added crime. Crime is nearly as disastrous as any of the other four and it causes many deaths. Like those of the underground economy, the consequences of crime are not measurable. We can measure the dollar cost of crime with considerable accuracy, but its true cost is in human misery and degradation, in frustration and cruelty and in corrosive erosion of all that is good in society, all that makes life worthwhile—and that cost cannot be measured.

We Americans have had more increase in crime in the past twenty-five years than in all the previous three hundred and more years of our history. President Reagan is the first occupant of the White House to be seriously concerned about the spread of crime. When Barry Goldwater was running for president, many persons laughed at his shrill demand for drastic steps to halt the spread of crime, but events have proved Goldwater was right. The Johnson, Nixon, Ford and Carter administrations and our state and local governments should have done much more than they

166

have to combat crime and reform our police, judicial and penal systems. The failure of our officials to act has caused the money loss from crime in the United States to rise to around $150 billion a year, about a three-fold increase in two decades. Of course, inflation accounts for a considerable part of this, but the actual incidence of murder, rape, violent assault, arson, armed robbery, burglary and all other crimes, both violent and non-violent, rose rapidly until about 1980. There has been a small drop in reported crimes during the first two years of the Reagan administration. The drop probably cannot be credited directly to active steps taken by the administration, but certainly the psychological climate set by the administration has had considerable to do with it.

The slight diminution of crime in the past two years has not yet had great social or economic impact. We still have to face the fact that the spread of crime has brought us to a social crisis almost as great as the slavery issue that brought on the Civil War. The streets in our big cities no longer are safe either at night or by day and most of us have to live and work behind locked doors. More small retail establishments in some cities are being forced out of business by crime than by the recession or inflation. Our police are undermanned and their hands often are virtually tied by stupid restrictions imposed at the behest of civil rights extremists.

In January, 1982, Judge Gabriel Kraussman of the Criminal Court of the City of New York said on a popular radio program that judges are virtually powerless to enforce the law or mete out justice under the present system—they cannot cope with the tactics of professional criminals and their unscrupulous lawyers, nor can they protect the innocent from being hailed before the courts unjustly on false charges brought by lazy, incompetent and dishonest store guards on shoplifting charges or on other malicious complaints.

For some years now, federal and local law enforcement officials have been insisting that not more than 5 percent of all the felonies and major misdemeanors committed in the United States are even reported to the authorities; people feel it doesn't do any good to report them. Of the crimes that are reported, fewer than 5 percent ever result in the apprehension of a suspect. That gives the average offender four-hundred-to-one odds against even being arrested on suspicion. These odds are not evenly spread. The more crimes an offender commits, the greater his chances of being ultimately apprehended, and the more serious a crime, the more concentrated attention it gets from the police and prosecuting attorneys and the greater chances there are of solving the crime and catching the criminal. The police have a pretty high batting average in catching murderers.

Nevertheless, the odds against conviction and punishment are staggering. Also in January, 1982, the Citizens Crime Commission of New York City presented statistics showing that only one in fourteen of those arrested ultimately was sentenced. Since the odds are four hundred to one against being arrested in the first place, that brings the total odds against being caught and punished for any given offense in New York City up to 5,600 to one!

The spread of crime has been an enormous stimulus to the growth of unemployment. Crime does this in two ways, first by appearing to be an easy, smart and attractive way to make a living, thus causing many persons to choose not to work regularly; and, secondly, by victimizing small business firms so continuously with robbery, burglary, extortion, vandalism and fraud that they quit business and fire their workers. Federal and local officials say there can be no doubt that the horrendous harassment of small businesses by professional criminals and teenage hoodlums has destroyed several million jobs in the United States in recent years.

If shopkeepers and professional persons such as physicians, dentists and even insurance agents who have to keep valuables in their offices are forced to live in ever-increasing fear of being killed or maimed in holdups or having their offices burglarized several times a year, they have little incentive to stay open long hours and hire extra workers. They have every incentive to curtail hours and lay off workers or even quit business. Since government figures show that small businesses normally provide half of all jobs, it is crystal clear that we never will solve the unemployment problem until we give small business more adequate protection against criminals.

Big business is hit by crime too. In fact, the gross monetary loss of big business to crime is much larger than that of small business, but crimes against big business are a bit less apt to involve violence and to cause a firm to give up and quit. But crime against big business firms forces costs up inordinately and may cut profit enough to cause large-scale layoffs.

The big odds against the offender's being caught and punished are really the heart of our crime problem. All historical experience proves that the only effective legal deterrent to crime is relative certainty of punishment. The relative severity of punishment plays only a minor role, and in the United States today punishment rarely is severe.

Before 1960 no one in America dared defend crime publicly. Now some clergymen and educators, many lawyers, civil rights militants and other self-proclaimed social messiahs shout that robbery, rape, arson, bombing, kidnapping and murder, even the invasion of a courtroom and the killing of a judge, may be mere justifiable dramatized political statements! We have seen these people openly inciting mobs to invade or bomb university, government and private offices and to burn down whole communities.

The mushrooming increase in drug addiction, which at last is starting to subside a little, is the most highly visible aspect of our crime problem. Drug addiction also is probably the biggest single cause of crime in the streets and the bloody strife between warring cliques of drug traffickers produces the most bizarre and most numerous gangland-style killings. Late in 1982, President Reagan launched a determined offensive against the drug traffic that held out the first real promise of success in some years. The change in social psychology, especially among young people, that began developing slowly at the end of the 1970s augured well for the success of Reagan's move. Although the traffic in marijuana, cocaine and some other dangerous drugs still was growing, youngsters of college age no longer appeared to consider heroin and other hard drugs to be the in thing.

But heroin remains a frightful scourge to the black community and to many others of the more deprived elements of American society. So does marijuana.

Cocaine is a dangerous drug, although it is not highly addictive and is a stimulant rather than a true narcotic. It is expensive and is used to a surprising degree by the well-to-do as well as by professional criminals. The traffic in cocaine is largely controlled by Latin Americans and the cocaine dealers wage murderous war among themselves in U.S. cities, resulting in many grisly killings. The Mafia appears to control the heroin traffic, while the marijuana business, the biggest trade of all, is divided among many criminal elements with Latin Americans possibly having the biggest share.

Unavoidably, the black civil rights movement has contributed somewhat to the toleration of crime. When many politicians and spokesmen for the federal government became concerned a few years back about the increase in crime in the streets they at once were attacked as racists by the militants and their academic and clerical allies. "They talk of crime in the streets but what they mean is Negro crime," the self-appointed messiahs shouted. "All this hue and cry about crime in the streets is just an excuse for imposing fascist repression on the blacks!"

Ironically, quite a number of the persons who trumpeted this nonsense the loudest have themselves been victims of crime in the streets and it is a statistical fact that blacks are the most frequent victims of street crime in the big cities. But any public official, judge or politician who raises his voice in favor of a sane return to law and order is at once denounced by the radicals as an incipient tyrant who puts law and order far above freedom and all the decent amenities. He is accused of being a sadist at heart because he wants to curb such amusements as mugging, bombing, arson, purse snatching, rape and wanton cop killing. Young and not so young radicals and dropouts justify themselves in committing every variety of larceny and swindle by claiming they are "ripping off" or "liberating" the loot from "the Establishment," which, they claim, has been robbing the common people for generations.

This widespread toleration of crime and criminals naturally erodes public, official and business morality. We are discovering that liberality and lenity carried to the point of license and near anarchy also are hypocritical and can be worse than traditional injustices. A climate of extreme lenience toward criminal behavior also leads inevitably to an erosion of all sense of civic duty, to a desire to evade taxes and military service, or to look the other way and refuse to uphold or help the authorities in the ordinary execution of public affairs.

There also has been an enormous change in attitudes in our country towards religion, parental authority, sexual preferences, contraception and abortion and other aspects of the life style. So we must not confuse our present repudiation of old-fashioned Puritanism with toleration of criminal behavior. We should keep firmly in mind just what activity really is criminal and anti-social.

Another thing that should concern us greatly is that, in a modern democracy, it is up to the people themselves to preserve a reasonable degree of law and order and social responsibility. It is extremely naïve to expect politicians who must stand for election and reelection in communities where even the most immature and irresponsible have the ballot, to take the lead in prescribing an acceptable life style. A Roman Caesar, a Chinese emperor or an eighteenth-century European monarch could influence public morals drastically and put a stop to an era of decadence and license by personal example and rigorous repression. In the past, the Catholic, Protestant and Jewish clergy could influence morals and manners strongly in the United States. But their power to do this has waned mightily in recent decades. The rise of broadcast evangelism may be restoring clerical influence somewhat.

Even in the communist countries, where the party chiefs can ordain moral and social codes, enforce them rigidly, change them at will and relax them, then clamp down again and impose a Red Puritanism on the people, the moral codes do not work unless they have popular support.

The ultimate cause of crime is not known.

On analysis, the deprivation theory asserted so confidently by some criminologists, sociologists, educators and politicians that crime results from poverty, ignorance, discrimination and oppression, cannot be proved. It becomes a glittering and unconvincing generalization. It does not stand up to the test of hard logic and it certainly does not stand up to the test of historical experience.

Much crime is associated inescapably with poverty, ignorance and discrimination. That most certainly explains why crime rates among blacks are higher than among whites in the United States. But you can find neighborhoods of poor blacks in this country where the crime rate is low and rich white neighborhoods where it is high. Crime is very rare among some of the most primitive tribes in Africa and extremely high and bizarre in some of the most affluent white communities in America.

A more plausible idea is that all crime is psychotic. Probably most crimes of violence and the habitual practice of burglary, larceny and swindling can be traced to psychopathic personality traits. But this theory does not sufficiently account for the most costly and largest class of crime—the so-called white-collar or business crimes such as graft and official corruption, chiseling and cheating in business, contract, tax and insurance frauds and unlawful and immoral monopolistic practices.

Even if we could accept a working hypothesis that all crime is psychotic, that wouldn't get us very far because, as a science, psychiatry still is in a very primitive state. The psychiatrists know very little about the real origins of mental or emotional disorders so, naturally, they can do very little about them. That is why our mental hospitals remain so crowded and why so many patients released from them fail to make it on the outside and soon return to these institutions, often after committing crimes. President Reagan narrowly escaped being killed by one of these psychopaths. His administration is initiating a study of how to change the legal application of the insanity defense in criminal trials to better protect society as well as the psychopath.

The greatest single advance in helping psychotic patients has been the discovery by pharmaceutical chemists of tranquilizing and stabilizing drugs. But these drugs do not attack the unknown causes of mental and emotional illness, they merely provide palliative treatment of the symptoms. The patient usually has to stay on the drugs indefinitely.

Alcoholism is associated with an enormous amount of crime but it certainly can't be called an ultimate cause of crime, and the ultimate cause or causes of alcoholism are no better known than those of mental and emotional illness; so alcoholism cannot be cured, it can only be arrested by abstinence.

Since all criminal behavior appears to be aggression, either directly or by stealth, against others, the ultimate cause of crime in human beings may be bound up with whatever trait it is in the human personality that makes us more aggressive and warlike than the lower animals.

But anthropologists, ethologists and other scientists are having no luck in identifying this trait. They are divided into arguing camps, those who contend that this passion for aggression is instinctive in the human race and another group that insists aggression is an environmental trait acquired by man in pre-historic times. This second group insists on the basis of rather flimsy evidence that aggression is by no means a common trait in mankind. But none of this speculation is of any practical help in combatting crimes.

It is much easier to observe criminal behavior in action than to try to determine its ultimate cause. The police and prosecutors depend largely on discovering the motivation for individual crimes and the methods of operation of habitual offenders in initial apprehension of offenders and in building evidence to get convictions in court. Particular crimes are motivated by many emotional drives: jealousy, revenge, greed, lust, sadism, ambition, blind rage and, most frequently of all, by panic.

Psychologists say much crime can be described as personal innovation, which is a fancy way of saying refusing to be bound by the rules of the game of life. Unable to win within the rules or imagining he can't win, the criminal innovates and makes his own rules. He then starts living in a jungle world of fantasy and keeps on making up the rules as he goes along to justify himself in any offense that will help him achieve his goals.

Even if the statistical incidence of crime diminished in the early 1980s, the nature of many crimes became more bizarre. There were more indiscriminate murders, more mass killings and more murders characterized by sadistic and fiendish cruelty. There were more callous and brazen extortion attempts, such as the plot to extort a huge sum from Gulf Oil Corporation in 1982 by a gang that planted bombs in one of the company's refineries. For sheer callous cruelty, nothing quite equals the indiscriminate lacing of Tylenol pain killer capsules with cyanide. This resulted quickly in seven persons being killed in the Chicago region. It is a commentary on the state to which the spread of crime had reduced public psychology that some persons suspected that the Tylenol poisoning was a plot to make a killing in the stock market by selling shares of the company that made the capsules short just before news of the deaths. One could hardly do that without leaving a trail, since short sales of listed stocks must be reported promptly. The company's shares did take a fearful battering on news of the cyanide deaths, and securities analysts said it would take the company years to recover from this blow dealt by someone who is obviously psychotic.

Curbing crime is a problem of the highest priority for every American, but it actually has to be done by the police and the courts and it is up to us to compel the politicians to give them the means and incentive to do the job.

It is an observable fact that the American public constantly exaggerates the shortcomings and sins of police officers. This goes back to our colonial forebears' desire to tolerate only the smallest possible number of police and the least authority that could be grudgingly extended. In Europe at that time, the police power was vested in the army and it was used wtih ruthless arrogance on the civilians. The American colonial authorities, reacting against the European system, insisted on civilian police under strictly local control and severely limited authority. As a result, brutal neglect for law enforcement and patronizing contempt for the policeman have appeared to be ingrained in the character of many Americans.

In no other country have the police generally been treated so niggardly and no other advanced nation has neglected the art and science of criminology as much as we. The result is that long odds against apprehension and punishment of criminal offenders do not prevail in European countries. In the communist countries, the police stand at the very top of the social and economic scale.

A measure of the neglect of the police by the federal, state and local governments is found in a report by the White House Crime Commission that, in 1967, the combined cost of all the police and sheriff's forces and state and federal law enforcement officers was $2.8 billion, and 85 percent of this was in salaries. Projecting that to 1982, with adjustments for inflation, we get a current total of perhaps $8 billion. But there are at least 400,000 working police officers, which would indicate an average gross annual pay of $20,000, but while senior police officers in the big cities earn much more, the general average may be $15,000 or less. That is by no means a good salary for a man supporting a wife and children in these times and it certainly doesn't seem like adequate pay for a dangerous vocation with a high mortality rate.

Obviously, the typical cop's wife must work for pay or he must moonlight on another job. It's no wonder that until the recession put so many people out of work, many police forces were having difficulty recruiting up to authorized strength. Some were forced to take high school dropouts with not very good IQ's. Of course, that did not apply to New York and a few other cities that pay cops rather well.

Until very recently, there were very few policemen in even the better paying departments with college educations or any special training for the work. The obvious necessity to make physical fitness the first requisite in choosing from among applicants intensified the situation in which a majority of policemen were lads who had not made especially good grades in high school.

The policeman's opportunities for advancement are very limited in all except the largest cities. What chance has a young cop to advance and what incentive has he to improve his professional training on a six-man force? His chief may be making no more than a garage mechanic and yet he is responsible for the safety of an entire community.

Another indication of the magnitude of our neglect of the police is that we have several individual corporations with more employees than all the police in the country and they are better paid.

Except in the largest cities, job security and vacations for police are apt to be substandard. Disability and pension protection is better but not up to the best in private industry. In their everyday work, policemen see pimps, dope pushers, numbers runners and other criminals making three to ten times as much as a cop can earn. They also learn early about alliances between crime and business, about big insurance frauds, wholesale executive pilferage and tax cheating and this does not increase their respect for humanity or their own self-esteem.

So it is obvious that police pay in all our smaller and middle-sized communities ought to be raised. In spite of the recession we can afford it because all police protection costs us only about forty dollars a year per capita.

Some persons are led to the false conclusion that a rapid expansion of police personnel would solve the national crime problem. Undoubtedly many cities and towns are seriously underpoliced, but adding a lot more men would not get at the real heart of the problem. The main problems of the police are lack of true sophistication and lack of scientific management techniques. The typical police chief runs a tight ship and is conscientious, but he probably is a hardnose with an instinct for local politics, who joined the force as a rookie right out of high school. His idea of innovation is a new model squad car or an improved radio transmitter. He may be a good disciplinarian and a good judge of men but he is certain to be completely naïve about modern managerial skills, and if he had a lot more men, they might be more of an encumbrance than a help to him.

If this sounds like a plea to turn a small army of Harvard Business School graduates loose on the country's police forces, forget it. Harvard has nothing to teach the cops as yet. Real administrative skills in police work don't exist in the United States now even in theory. The English have them and so do the French and so do the communist countries, but we can't borrow them. Their principles are applicable only to totally centralized national police forces and they could not be made to work in our crazy-quilt, fragmented system.

We have made a fumbling start toward developing police managerial skills. Every state now has some kind of program and many policemen are taking degree courses to move up a few notches in the civil service but often the courses offered by the state schools consist of little more than bureaucratic and pedagogical gobbledegook. The FBI and our state police forces have yet to astonish or impress the public with their effectiveness. Nevertheless, it probably would make considerable sense to turn over the police functions of villages, towns and rural counties to the state police. The state cops would not protect school kids crossing the streets or issue parking tickets or summonses for improper rubbish disposal, but they would do all the investigation of felonies and major misdemeanors.

Recruiting and training young people to become good professional police officers still would not be easy. Fewer than one hundred of our colleges and universities offer any courses in police science, and these courses are not backed up by any proven record of performance or accomplishment. There isn't much incentive for youngsters entering college to take them.

The lack of sophistication and training in police work actually applies more to the higher officers than to cops or plainclothes detectives pounding the streets or riding squad cars. Too many of the superiors owe their rank entirely to political pull both inside and outside the department, and that's what they devote their efforts to. On the other hand, the working patrolmen and detectives, in spite of their educational handicaps, often reveal a remarkable degree of hard-nosed sophistication in their work. They develop remarkable skills, acquire enviable stores of knowledge and reveal fertile imaginations in developing and using techniques for solving crimes and tracking down offenders. And the overwhelming majority have an admirable sense of devotion to duty. The traditional "by the book" methods developed through generations of toil by patient, hard working officers are very sound and often achieve very great results. So does the work of the forensic laboratories, the fingerprint and identification bureaus, the missing persons bureaus and the keepers of computerized cross-indexed files of offenders by their prior records, methods of operation and other important characteristics.

However, much of work expected of policemen is beyond their training and skills and much of what they are asked to do is actually beneath their skills and stultifying. As a result, many policemen seem either frustrated and confused or bored with their jobs. Writing parking tickets, getting a cat down from a tree or ticketing people for untidy lawns is degrading to a policeman. Long hours spent on stake-out duty are boring but at least the officer knows it is necessary and could pay off in an important arrest. But parking tickets and school crossing duty are for the birds. Why can't they be left to retirees and the auxiliaries?

Policemen are called out frequently to stop fights between husbands and wives or between parents and adolescent children. Thousands of officers are wounded and some are killed when they blunder on these assignments. Government records indicate nine or ten cops are killed on such duty every year.

Now what is there in the education or training of the average policeman to equip him to stop drunken, psychotic or furiously jealous husbands and wives from beating or killing each other? Or enraged fathers and sons? If the officer attempts to use force he may have to kill someone or he may be killed. The cop who is stabbed by a wife while trying to arrest the husband who has just given her a savage beating is an old story in police squad rooms.

If we could get improved and scientific management in police departments, the benefits undoubedtly would be substantial. There would be better deployment of manpower, probably less paperwork for officers, better arrest procedures and less waste of time on arraignments and other court appearances by police officers that aren't really necessary (the officers might present routine testimony by remote television, for example). There could be more centralized booking procedures, quicker and more thorough investigations of incidents involving disputed arrests that arouse resentment in the neighborhood and the creation of the savage emotional waves that can lead to rioting. Much taxpayers' money might also be saved by better police management techniques.

However, it would be naïve to think that better police management of itself could have a big impact in solving the nation's crime problems. That is still up to the public, our educators, our politicians and above all to the criminal courts.

The shortcomings of our criminal courts and our criminal lawyers are infinitely worse than those of the police, and these shortcomings all are ingrained in the system. We have an adversary judicial system in which two sides fight the issues out before a judge or a judge and jury. In civil suits this works reasonably well because the civil suit trial normally is about only money and property, not life or liberty, and so is a relatively unemotional debate. But when a criminal case goes to a full-scale trial in one of our courts it is only an extension of medieval trial by battle: the superstition that God will aid the champion of the right. But in truth, both the contest between knights in armor and the battle of wits between lawyers never were and are anything but contests of naked power having nothing to do with justice.

Our present criminal trial system did not derive directly from medieval trial by battle. The clash of knights armed with sword and buckler to decide the guilt or innocence of the accused was only an alternative to the harsh style of administered justice inherited from the Romans, and the present system of trial by attorney adversaries also developed as an alternative to the harsh administered justice systems of authoritarian monarchs. The present system is only three hundred years old and less than that in the United States. Colonial justice in our country was administered, and it was harsh and arbitrary. There was no real presumption of the innocence of the accused. There was no bail, and judges often doubled as prosecutors. There were no court-appointed defense attorneys and the government would bear no expense on behalf of the accused.

The defendant was obliged to testify in his own behalf and enjoyed no immunity against self-incrimination. Nearly half of all persons accused of crime died of jail fever and other infectious diseases while awaiting trial. But this system was not without its merits. It was swift and punishment of the guilty was certain. The temper of the times in both England and the colonies was that even the rich and powerful were likely to go to the gallows once they were hailed into court.

Our modern trial by battle is a great improvement over that, but it still is a farce and a hoax. It is founded on a legal fiction, a proposition that is manifestly untrue. This fiction is the notion that the truth inevitably will emerge from a contest of the powers of deception and persuasion between the opposing lawyers.

Since this proposition is palpably false, it cannot result in justice and it ought to be discarded now.

We can take it for granted that the lawyers will not willingly discard this hypocritical system, and candor compels us to admit that trial by battle has lasted because no one has thought of anything better to take its place. But today we have the tools, if we will only set our minds to using them, to create a more scientific legal and judicial system that will seek only to discover the truth. Such a system still could be based on the presumption of innocence although there is no real logical basis for this time-honored presumption. But it would *not* be based on the naked power plays and bare-faced hypocrisies of the adversary system. A lawyer no longer would be allowed to plead a defendant innocent whom he knows full well to be guilty.

Lawyers rightly contend that they alone have been responsible for the steady improvement of judicial systems since Roman times. But their efforts all have been in one direction, towards a climate of leniency and towards systems giving tremendous power and profit to the legal profession. So it is naïve to expect lawyers to accept what is patent to laymen, that the climate of lenity the lawyers have created has become an intolerable burden to humanity and criminal trial attorneys have become irresponsible parasites preying on society.

This is not new to the world. It happened in ancient Rome and helped to destroy Roman civilization. Many historians have noted that in all the days of the Roman republic and the empire, the Romans never were so fond of litigation and never were so boastful of their meticulous and scrupulous observance of the forms of the law as during the years when the whole of Roman society was crumbling into decadence. The rise in crime in the United States today and mushrooming decadence in American society also coincide with a meticulous regard for the legal niceties and legal forms such as civilization never before has encountered. The rights of criminals are considered far more important than the rights of society.

Our courts, the criminal trial lawyers and the law schools are becoming the tools and allies of the criminals.

Nevertheless, the trouble with our criminal courts is not so much with their procedure as with the motivation of the opposing lawyers. The blunt fact is that neither the defense counsel nor the prosecutor has any incentive to discover the truth about what happened. Defense counsel is interested only in winning an acquittal or, failing that, in getting a lenient sentence for his or her client.

It is common to hear a defense lawyer stand up pompously before the jury and roar: "I am just as much an officer of this court as the District Attorney or His Honor the Judge. I am sworn to uphold the law just as they are and to tell you, ladies and gentlemen, only the strictest truth!"

But outside the courtroom, and even in the courtroom, the same lawyer will declaim with equal fervor that his sole duty is to his client, to keep him out of prison, and to admit that he will suppress evidence or distort it in order to do so. So he lied when he said he would uphold the law and tell the jury only the strictest truth. His pretense to being a dedicated officer of the court is pure hypocrisy. Criminal trial lawyers are not supposed to lie to the judge or to the jury or to persuade witnesses to perjure themselves. In truth, they do so habitually. Judges expect them to and rarely make any effort to punish them for it.

The motives of the prosecutors often are quite as reprehensible. The first concern of the average prosecutor is neither to establish the truth and see that justice is done nor to mete out punishment as a deterrent. The prosecutor's real concerns are his personal political, economic and social ambitions and the burdens of his job. He weighs every trial and every issue in terms of how it will affect *him*, not in terms of how it will affect the accused or society.

Although lawyers praise trial by battle they are quick enough to abandon it in favor of arbitration or administrative procedures whenever they can do so profitably. They are as eager to make deals with the district attorney on behalf of a client as the accused is to get a lesser conviction without trial. If he cannot make a satisfactory deal, the defense lawyer's next ploy still is to avoid trial. He is well aware that a trial is only a contest of will and wits between him and the prosecutor and that anything can happen in the courtroom or in the jury room. A lucky blow by the prosecutor or by a persuasive juror while the veniremen are trying to reach a verdict can bring counsel's defense tumbling down like a house of cards and send his client to prison. So he tries to avoid trial as long as he can.

The strategy of delay continues even after trial and conviction. Chief Justice Warren Burger has inveighed over and over again against the ease with which our system allows attorneys to win multiple trials and press multiple appeals over a period that may last ten years, even when every judge and every juror involved is well aware of the guilt of the defendant. We won't begin to solve our crime problem until something is done to put a halt to long delays and frivolous appeals.

Perhaps we should have a constitutional amendment forbidding all appeals on technical grounds, allowing appeals only on plausible new evidence that may establish the innocence of the accused beyond a reasonable doubt.

Procedure based on dubious legal dogmas founded on pyramided precedents is more sacred than justice in our courts. It is considered vastly more important to obey the dogmas than to protect society against criminals, and since the dogmas were developed by lawyers and perfected by the repeated citing of precedents, it is not surprising that all the dogmas are designed to make the law more lenient in practice and to make it easier for defense lawyers to win cases and earn fees. This has been in the past of great benefit to the common man. But now we have reached a point where these legal dogmas make it horribly easy for unscrupulous lawyers to shy away from the unpleasant facts in the evidence and keep the prosecution in a criminal trial off balance by a vast array of technical fencing tactics drawn from the pyramided precedents.

One of the oldest and worst of these dogmas is that only an ignorant jury can be impartial. Jurors are forbidden to make any inquiry of any kind on their own and are bound to only what the lawyers choose to tell them or let the witnesses tell them about the case. An example of the mischief this absurd notion can cause occurred a few years ago in a case of child murder in New York. One of the jurors visited the scene of the crime in the evening to satisfy himself about the physical plausibility of some of the evidence and the defense got a mistrial as a result after the jury had returned the verdict of guilty. On retrial a second conviction was obtained but a vast amount of time and taxpayers' money was wasted. If a vital witness had died meanwhile the prosecutor might have had to abandon the case.

This rule that jurors (and even judges) be ignorant of the facts and circumstances at issue in a criminal trial is at the very heart of the failings of our judicial system. When trial by jury first became prevalent in England in the thirteenth century, succeeding trial by compurgation (the combined oaths of a number of leading citizens of the community that they believed the accused either to be guilty or to be innocent), there was no requirement that jurors be ignorant of the case or that they not seek information about it on their own. On the contrary, the practice was the exact opposite of what it is today. Jurors were chosen precisely because they knew the accused and the accuser and were familiar with the facts surrounding the case and hence could come quickly to a decision. This is the way private justice still is conducted in the family, in the school and on the job.

Early in 1982, the Citizens Crime Commission of New York took an indignant stand against the manipulation of juries by lawyers in our courts. The commission found it took two and a half days on the average (it often takes much longer) to pick a jury for a trial in the criminal courts of New York. The corresponding time in the federal courts was two hours. The commission noted that lawyers rather than judges have come to control the process of choosing juries and it called for a new system that would give judges complete control over the choice of jurors and exclude the lawyers from the process. That makes good sense.

In late years, many absurdities regarding the admissibility or inadmissibility of testimony have been successfully insinuated into our court procedural rules by the machinations of unscrupulous lawyers. As a result, we have departed from the sound practice of the courts in England. The most serious of these changes was the adoption of the policy that evidence obtained in violation of the constitutional restrictions on search and seizure is tainted permanently and totally and must not be allowed to be presented in court. The theory is that the admission of tainted evidence is a violation of the due process clause of the fourteenth amendment.

This is tortuous and pernicious reasoning. It does not punish those officers who obtain evidence illegally but it frequently allows the guilty to go free, thus punishing society instead of the offender.

Under the English rule that could not happen.

The tainted evidence rule has been carried to even more absurd lengths. Even if the tainted evidence is not offered in court, the fact that the police obtained evidence illegally might be used subsequently to void a conviction, even in the face of overwhelming proof of guilt.

There are other dogmatic legal absurdities that have been grafted on to our judicial system by the lawyers over the years that make things a lot easier for the professional criminal and his cunning, unscrupulous attorney. These deal with cross-examination of the defendant, pretrial disclosure of the prosecution's case, the erosion of the judges' power to comment on the meaning of the evidence and the practice of trying a criminal on only one offense when he is accused of a whole string of offenses and forbidding any reference to the other offenses in the trial. This last prevents the prosecution from giving the judge and jury a true picture of the nature of the defendant and his crimes. These dogmas are pretended to be measures to protect the defendant's natural civil rights; in fact, they are only mechanisms built up over the years by lawyers to thwart justice and cheat society for their own profit.

Although Professor Gutman says the cost of crime is only a quarter to a third of the total cost of the underground economy, its price in things more important than money is so enormous that we cannot hope to save America without winning the struggle against crime.

The Reagan administration has shown a lot more determination to wage an intelligent and wide-front war on crime than any other in recent decades.

IX

Exports and the Welfare State

THE UNITED STATES never again can be a self-sufficient nation; we have used up too many of our once abundant natural resources. And we never again can dominate world trade as we did in the years immediately following World War II.

Our future, even our survival, depends on exporting and in the past decade we have done nothing to assure that we will be able to expand our exports. Indeed we have done many things to raise doubts about our ability to export and survive. President Reagan is striving mightily to reverse the tragic trend of the past decade, and on October 8, 1982, he signed into law a bill that eventually could prove to be a landmark and a turning point in our dismal foreign trade record of recent years.

This bill is the Export Trading Company Act, the purpose of which is to make it vastly easier for thousands of American companies to sell their products in overseas markets. And for the first time in our history it will become possible to export professional services such as engineering, architecture, accounting, insurance and financial counseling, legal services, etc., along with merchandise and capital equipment, in single packages.

186

It will take some years for American manufacturers, commercial companies and financial institutions to set up enough export trading companies under the new law to wield a big effort in reversing our current unfavorable foreign trade balance. But getting the new law enacted may well be one of the most important economic achievements of this century.

Under the enabling legislation signed by Mr. Reagan, a number of factors that traditionally have hindered the potential of U.S. exporters are seriously dealt with for the first time. The new law grants protection from antitrust prosecution for joint enterprises and new authority for bank holding companies, bankers' banks and Edge Act subsidiaries of bank holding companies to invest directly in export trading companies (ETCs).

The act is designed to encourage various entities to become involved with ETCs either as investors or suppliers of goods and services. Such entities may include banks, insurance companies, other financial institutions, large multinational corporations, manufacturers and suppliers, transportation and shipping companies, retailers, wholesalers, jobbers and government-sponsored corporations such as port authorities and economic development agencies.

The typical ETC envisioned by the new law will be "essentially a middleman between the U.S. supplier and the foreign purchaser," explains Allen Weltmann, a Washington partner in Coopers Lybrand, the big national accounting firm. "We see a typical ETC as basically a one-stop shop providing a full range of export services to American business," Weltmann added. Those services include marketing, export-related insurance, legal assistance, foreign currency exchange, financing and product research and design.

Weltmann said the ETC could either take title to export products or act as a commissioned agent: "For a U.S. company, exporting goods through an ETC could be similar to a domestic sale."

The new legislation is unique in that it neither imposes burdensome regulatory restrictions nor does it require any

federal spending. "As we see it, "Weltmann said, "by less-
ening present trade barriers, the new law will open the
door for the first time to potential exporters who have the
foresight to move ahead in this area."

Of course, the Japanese have been using big export trading companies for decades. All their big industrial com-
bines, Mitsubishi, Mitsui and others, operate huge export
trading companies all over the world.

In spite of his achievement in accepting the Export Trading Company Act and getting it passed, Mr. Reagan so far
has had precious little understanding and cooperation from
American business in the matter of foreign trade. American
management seems to have been mesmerized into a combination of frightened frustration and soft-headed compla-
cency ever since the first Arab oil embargo of 1973–74.
The energy crisis became an excuse for productivity failure, failure to export and every kind of failure in management. Why this should have been so is a mystery, because
the United States was hurt much less by the recurring energy crises than other advanced industrial countries. Japan
already had shown the world in the 1960s that shortages of
energy and raw materials can be overcome by managerial
skill, technology, science and national unity and devotion
to purpose.

The energy problem is subsiding. Oil, gas and coal are
expensive but there is enough of them now and it is pretty
clear that before the end of this century the world no longer will depend on oil. The supply of energy will become
unlimited. Nuclear fusion will replace nuclear fission and
produce unlimited electricity and hydrogen. Sea thermal
energy also may be fairly widely utilized. And recently two
breakthroughs have been intimated, although not proven
by sustained performance tests, in the direct extraction of
hydrogen from water at reasonable cost. Oil will be needed, but as petrochemical feedstock, not as fuel.

But we cannot count on the availability of unlimited energy to restore industry's productivity automatically to the
former levels of our days of economic glory. On the contrary, it could have the opposite effect because, unlike pe-
troleum and coal, these new sources of energy would be-

come available to practically the whole world. We still will be up against the competitive factors that have us buffaloed now. We Americans will be even more dependent on our own intelligence and industry to survive than we are at present. In fact, unless we change our present economic and social strategies drastically, we and the other welfare states in the North Atlantic region are likely to go into economic decline, because we will be increasingly unable to compete with the high productivity-oriented nations of East Asia. We also will have trouble competing with the communist countries because, although they also are welfare states, their governments are very austerity-minded and keep the brakes tight on wages and other production and social costs.

The North Atlantic welfare state countries are not re-investing enough in industry because their present levels of individual savings are too low to permit raising large amounts of new equity capital. Too much money in these countries is diverted to subsidized consumption in the form of high wages and social benefits. High progressive income taxes, declining labor discipline, poor labor mobility—neither workers nor executives want to accept transfers—health insurance programs so generous in some European countries that workers can be absent from the job at practically no cost to themselves, and very high unemployment benefits, often awarded illegally without sensible controls, reduce production in these welfare state countries and seriously diminish their ability to compete in world markets.

On the other hand, Harvard Business School Professor Bruce Scott writes,* "the Japanese have shaped their policies in housing, banking and social welfare to support a strategy of raising the standard of living by raising savings, investment and productivity. Labor policy is part of the strategy. Lifetime employment in large companies means employees share in the productivity gains instead of being displaced by them."

Scott adds, "We cannot achieve long-term economic re-

*Harvard Business Review, September–October, 1982.

covery as long as U.S. policy focuses on short-term consumer welfare and on the entitlements and subsidies of a welfare state. This policy has steadily shifted American economic incentives away from work, saving and investment."

He notes that the Japanese strategy requires a high level of investment, hence a high level of savings. "Rejecting western ideas of heavy borrowing or inviting foreign capital participation, the Japanese have chosen to finance their investment from domestic savings and have been saving 20 percent of personal disposable income a year as against only 5 percent in the United States."

A complete book on this subject of the decline of western productivity due to the rise of the top-heavy welfare state and the rapid development of the southeast Asian countries as a competitive threat appeared in the summer of 1982. It is entitled *The Eastasia Edge* (Basic Books, New York, 1982) and was written by Professor Kent E. Calder of Harvard and Roy Hofheinz, Jr., president of Hofheinz World Trade, Incorporated. Calder and Hofheinz take much the same view of the matter as Professor Scott, but seem to be more alarmed by the situation. They say that if U.S. companies are to compete successfully against the rising economic tide surging from "Eastasia," our political leaders are going to have to take immediate and drastic steps. They say we clearly are in a moment of deadly crisis but that "we do not act as though we appreciated the dangers at hand."

This book says our whole economic view of the world has become cockeyed and that we must alter many of our present ideas and, most specifically, our tax policies.

It is not just Japan we must worry about, but the other east Asian countries whose economies have been growing much faster than ours—Taiwan, mainland China, South and North Korea, Hong Kong and Singapore. These countries are becoming dominant in the world in some high-technology industries. For example, Japan has 70 percent of the market for industrial robotics that will reach about $2 billion a year by 1990, yet the first successful industrial robots were made in the United States. Fifteen of the fifty largest banks in the world now are east Asian and, since 1975, the transpacific trade of the United States has been more important than our transatlantic trade, with the east Asian countries having big surpluses in much of the trade at our expense.

Calder and Hofheinz warn that we Americans cannot cope with the rise of east Asian economic might by resorting to our traditional weapon, the high protective tariff. They say high tariffs against east Asian products would only cause renewed inflation in the United States and, in the long run, would cause more American unemployment by further reducing our ability to compete abroad. We simply cannot isolate our economy successfully as we thought we were doing in the high tariff heydays of the nineteenth century and the first third of this century.

Calder and Hofheinz say bluntly that Japanese steelmakers found that U.S. quotas on their products helped them to keep their prices artificially high in the American market, thus passing on the higher prices to steel consumers. They also evaded the quotas to some extent by selling steel in the United States through German mills. The U.S. auto companies, the largest customers for Japanese steel, were forced to raise prices of their cars, then compete against Japanese cars built with cheap Japanese steel in Japan. Import quotas on special steels in 1976 similarly gave Japan and Korea the chance to grab the U.S. market for bearings.

The quota agreement in 1977 on television receivers did indeed cut imports of Japanese TV sets but it didn't halt the drop in employment in the U.S. television manufacturing industry. The U.S. companies still had to move their production abroad in order to get wages down so they could compete.

The 1981 voluntary restraints on Japanese automobile exports to the United States didn't work. They merely prodded the Japanese automakers into sending more advanced and more exotic cars to America.

Calder and Hofheinz find additionally that the problem of what to do about the east Asian trade menace is complicated by the fact that American companies now have such a major stake in the east Asian trade. "Virtually all the large

U.S. electronics manufacturers, General Electric, RCA and even Zenith (which led the political fight against alleged Japanese dumping of television sets in America during the 1970s) have moved the bulk of their consumer electronics production to east Asia," Calder and Hofheinz write. These American firms supply the U.S. and other markets from their east Asian plants.

Calder and Hofheinz add that "a growing proportion of the private brand merchandise American sundry stores stock, including many of the small appliances sold under such labels as Sears Roebuck's Kenmore brand, also is made in east Asia. They say large American banks also have a big stake in the east Asian trade growth, so do American controlled multinational corporations who act on the old maxim, "If you can't lick 'em, join 'em." This is particularly attractive to the banks because, in contrast to western Europe, where international trade is largely in local currencies, 90 percent of east Asia's fast-growing trade is in U.S. dollars. The big American retailing chains also find east Asian products extremely advantageous because the east Asian manufacturers allow higher profit margins to American distributors and dealers on the average than American manufacturers. This increases their edge in U.S. markets.

American raw materials producers in such states as Montana, Oregon and Washington also have a huge stake in the east Asia trade.

Although the east Asian production and trade phenomenon undoubtedly is the biggest single factor in unemployment in Detroit, Calder and Hofheinz do not believe the further growth of east Asian trade with the United States will cause anywhere near as much American unemployment as the scale of the trade might suggest. The reason they feel this way is that east Asian imports are concentrated in a few fields—steel, automobiles, electronics and clothing—and the east Asians usually try to find gaps in the U.S. markets rather than risk a head-on collision with domestic producers. The great success of Japanese motorcycles in America is an example of this. The motorcycle was an extremely marginal product in the United States until the Japanese took it up and popularized it with a wide range of new glamorous models.

As Calder and Hofheinz see it, it is the failure of U.S. manufacturers to produce and export sensibly rather than the success of the east Asians in our country that we should worry about. Also, Calder and Hofheinz say we cannot meet the east Asian challenge by copying their methods. "Copying Eastasia uncritically would be frustrating as well as potentially dangerous," they say, "since the most fundamental reasons for Eastasian economic success are not transferable. Eastasian society, from Japan to China to Singapore, took centuries to evolve and works together only in the aggregate."

But, they conceded, we can learn some things from the east Asians—Japanese quality control, Korean worker motivation and some aspects of Chinese technology. However, what we can learn most from the east Asians is how to run our own society on the basis of cooperation instead of confrontation, with government, management and labor working together and not against each other.

Calder and Hofheinz do not fail to note that, except for mainland China, North Korea and Vietnam, east Asia depends heavily on the American defense umbrella and hence does not have to spend much on its own defense.

As for what we Americans must do to avoid being overwhelmed by the east Asian challenge, Professor Scott says we should copy the Japanese in one respect: long-term commitment of big companies to their workers. He says industrial performance in the United States will improve when employers give economic security through long-term commitments to workers in productive, profitable companies. Like Scott, Calder and Hofheinz are very critical of the American tax system. They say it discourages investment in industrial expansion and modernization. Contrarily, they say, the east Asian tax systems compel saving and promote what is called "the creative destruction" of existing plants to make room for new plants and more innovative manufacturing to get higher value-added production. The United States needs to re-examine its present investment tax credit policy seriously, because the price of a poor tax policy is not that one part of society will benefit at the expense of another but that all sectors will lose out to more efficient outsiders.

Calder and Hofheinz note that in general in east Asian countries, only one-fifth of the Gross National Product is absorbed by taxes, whereas in the United States the amount taken out by taxes is nearly one-third of the GNP. And they say that, on the average, Europe and North America spend more than four times as much of their national incomes on welfare as east Asia. They say this difference in tax and welfare burdens is about the biggest reason that unemployment in east Asia generally is less than 4 percent of the working force.

An even more critical measurement of the failure of American business management to increase productivity and halt the decline in our competitive position in the world is made by Arnold S. Judson, a Boston management consultant, in an article entitled "The Awkward Truth About Productivity" in the *Harvard Business Review* for September–October, 1982.

Judson implies rather bluntly that American managers do not care enough about productivity, that they don't want to make the best use of office workers and knowledge workers and don't pay much attention to the critical interactions of such functions as product engineering with manufacturing and marketing. He says a recent survey of 236 top-level executives in 195 companies showed that more than half had productivity gains of less than 5 percent a year, and 25 percent of the executives couldn't even measure their companies' productivity. What was worse, Judson said, many of those who claimed productivity gains hadn't adjusted their figures for inflation and didn't realize that their productivity actually had fallen.

He said that, in spite of all the talk about productivity gains, most American efforts to achieve such gains are half-hearted and ill-founded for the following reasons:

—They are too narrow and are concerned only with cost cutting.
—They are disjointed and aimed at curing visible symptoms and not at finding the real causes of low productivity.

—They are nearly always too short-term—less than one year. Too many executives are interested only in "quick fixes."
—Few companies have any specific or detailed plans for achieving productivity gains.
—Chief executives rarely get involved in productivity planning. They leave it up to plant managers.

Judson considers this last the most serious failing. The chief executive not only fails to get personally involved in the struggle to achieve productivity, he doesn't delegate the matter to another "sponsor" executive and give him or her the authority and facilities to push productivity vigorously and intelligently either on an overall basis or in specific projects.

Judson didn't write about the east Asians, but Professor Scott and Calder and Hofheinz made it plain that east Asians are doing the things Judson accuses American managers of not doing.

During 1982, the strength of the U.S. dollar against foreign currencies made exporting more difficult for many American firms because it made prices of American goods high in local currencies abroad. But history shows such currency problems can be overcome by good management and technology. The U.S. dollar has been strong in international markets throughout most of our history, yet American goods were very much in demand because they were of high quality, technologically advanced and were available promptly. West Germany has been able to expand its exports consistently in recent decades in spite of the fact that the German mark is strong against all currencies, including our dollar.

Ironically, in some markets, the big complaint against American goods is that they are underpriced, not overpriced, and in consequence there is not sufficient profit margin in them to satisfy foreign distributors and dealers.

European, Japanese and Third World trade experts say that the biggest reason why U.S. exports are not as large as they should be is that we don't try hard enough in world markets. In the first place, most American business firms do not realize how profitable export trade is and consider it too difficult. It is a matter of record that fewer than 10 percent of all American manufacturers make any effort to export their products. Most foreign international trade experts say thousands of American firms could sell on the world markets if they would try. The Commerce Department in Washington agrees that vastly more American businesses, especially small businesses, could export if they would try. Commerce has successfully persuaded many American firms of all sizes to enter the export markets in recent years.

The most common complaints about American export goods, other than their low prices, are:

—U.S. manufacturers refuse to take the trouble to tailor their products to suit the needs and tastes of peoples in individual countries, especially the Third World countries.

—American manufacturers won't learn the trading customs and distribution patterns of foreign lands and seek rather arrogantly to impose American practices on customers in these countries.

—American credit terms generally are too severe to be acceptable in countries where people have been used to longer, easier terms for generations.

—American manufacturers don't allow sufficient agents' commissions.

—Substantial gratuities that are regarded as legitimate in many countries are considered bribery under American law even if paid on foreign soil. This leads to embarrassments and scandals, since the people who get the gratuities often are well-connected politically.

—American business firms do not appreciate the value of long-term personal relationships in export trade.

—American goods have lost much of their technological edge in recent years.

—American tax laws impose double taxation on Americans who live abroad often and this keeps American manufacturers from keeping good people abroad to push exports and service export accounts.

—U.S. antitrust laws make it difficult to put together large international trade packages and trading groups that can act swiftly. Thus, the nation does not apply its full economic weight to foreign trade. The new Export Trading Company Act is the first comprehensive effort to deal with this problem.

Calder and Hofheinz say many large American-controlled multinational companies do very well in international trade but the flaw in their success from the point of view of the ordinary American is that the multinationals are much too willing and quick to move their production abroad, leaving American workers unemployed and American communities bereft of their plants. Calder and Hofheinz say the tax laws should be changed to compel the multinationals to export more and invest less abroad.

Not every aspect of east Asian economic policy is as deserving of commendation as Calder and Hofheinz appear to believe. The Japanese and some of the other east Asian countries clearly have engaged in aggressive and illegal dumping of products on the U.S. market at prices much below cost in order to get a foot in the door and eventually grab a major share of the market from American producers. What is worse, some of the east Asian states, particularly Hong Kong, have engaged in brazen and blatant pirating of American and other western patents and copyrights for sophisticated small electronic appliances and components, many processes and musical recordings and films, and have flooded world markets, including the U.S. market, with counterfeits and imitations.

One aspect of President Reagan's policies has had a serious adverse impact on our foreign trade. His sanctions against the Soviet pipeline to bring natural gas from Siberia to western Europe in retaliation for naked Soviet aggression against Afghanistan and the brutal Russian intervention in Poland against the Solidarity union movement are based on sound morality, but morality has little to do with such pragmatic matters as international trade in legitimate merchandise and equipment. Mr. Reagan's attempt to prevent the sale of American-engineered equipment for the Soviet pipeline not only failed, it caused deep resentment in western Europe. It caused American companies to lose some valuable contracts in Russia and generally has hurt the credibility of both the United States government and American business firms throughout the world.

For one thing, the Europeans do not accept at face value Mr. Reagan's moral indignation. His critics are inclined to think his real motive is to help the international oil companies to retain their west European markets.

Of course, although this short-term impact of Mr. Reagan's pipeline sanctions is serious, the long-term effect cannot yet be predicted. Various things could happen to put the president's policy in a better light.

X

A Place to Lay Your Head

WHEN I WAS GROWING UP in New York City, May 1 and October 1 were moving days.

Every year tens of thousands of New York families moved at the end of spring or in early autumn. They moved for an infinite variety of reasons: to get a little more room or because they needed less space, to get a more prestigious address or to economize, to be closer to work or to get farther out where there was more greenery, to be near a desirable school or church, to be closer to relatives and friends or to get away from relatives and neighbors who had become nuisances, to be closer to a park where the kids could play, to be near a public golf course or within easy distances of the many bays and canals in the city limits where one could keep a boat or get in an hour of bridge or rowboat fishing. Some people were willing to stand the roar of the El and subway trains just to be close to the Manhattan theatre district.

It was much the same in a lot of the rest of the country. Most families moved around; some frankly were fleeing their creditors, others were trying to make a new start in life and leave mistakes behind. Most were trying to better themselves in one way or another. But the reasons why families and individuals moved a lot in the 1920s and 1930s are not nearly so interesting as the all-important fact that they could move easily and almost at a moment's notice.

That is not possible today in most of America, and the fact that it isn't is an important measurement of what is wrong in the country. Our society lacks physical mobility and this is beginning to affect the upward social mobility and even the incentive to upward mobility of millions of persons in spite of our greater educational opportunities. It also is creating grave disruptions in industry and trade.

Most young people today probably find it hard to believe when their grandparents tell them that in the 1920s and 1930s a family could get off a train or drive into any city or village in America in the morning and find an affordable and reasonably satisfactory apartment by nightfall. Chances were that if the family had a thousand dollars in the bank they even could find an affordable and satisfactory house to buy within a few days and could get a mortgage quickly. What was difficult then was to sell a house, not to buy one if you had a little money. But often you had to take a loss to sell a house unless you were very patient about it.

What is more important is that this easy availability of affordable rental shelter varying from furnished rooms to full-sized houses had been standard in American communities almost from the beginnings of the country. Then as now people cared a lot about where they lived and sought comfortable, convenient quarters, and anyone who had a job or an income never had to worry about finding a place to lay his or her head at night under any circumstances. When one was faced with the prospect of taking a job in another city or town the last thing to be concerned about was finding living quarters. Rental shelter was so abundant in America that hardly anyone gave the matter of finding an apartment or a house even a passing thought in reaching a decision about a job.

Although the Great Depression of the 1930s caused a slump in building, the surplus of housing in the country was so large it took years for population growth to catch up with it. Not until the millions of soldiers and sailors came home from World War II, married, and began looking for homes did a real shortage develop. A housing boom then started, and with no inflation and mortgage money cheap, many millions of new houses and apartment buildings were put up in a hurry by private enterprise. But because Congress had voted rather liberal mortgage subsidies and other benefits to the veterans under the GI Bill of Rights, there was much more emphasis on building houses to sell than on building new rental housing.

Some subsidized public housing had been put up in the 1930s and a great deal more went up after the war. The Roosevelt administration had created the FHA-guaranteed level payment installment mortgage more to make homes more affordable to working class people and make surplus housing more salable than to encourage housing construction.

Owning a home became the goal of far more Americans after World War II than ever had been the case in the past. Indeed, before World War II many Americans considered owning your own home a foolish luxury and rarely a good investment. That also must sound strange to today's young Americans who have seen the prices of houses skyrocket so much that a home now is considered about the best investment a couple can make.

In point of fact, because of the high prices of homes today, selling one still can be difficult. As a rule, it's easy enough to find several persons who would like to buy the houses, but it's hard to find a buyer who can come up with the down payment and get a big enough and affordable mortgage. The rates are sky high, 11 to over 16 percent in recent years. In the late 1950s you could get a mortgage, even on an older house, at 5 percent or less.

The boom in home buying that began after World War II was accompanied initially by a boom in apartment house building, but it didn't provide rental housing fast enough to meet the demand and the federal government and the cities stepped in to fill the void with huge public housing projects. These projects have been anything but unqualified successes. In fact, many persons consider public housing in the United States an outright failure. The projects are too big to be easily manageable or even to be adequately maintained and policed. Their construction and their operation and management have resulted in numerous scandals. The main problems with them are that there are an enormous number of bureaucratic restrictions and restraints on getting into them, and politics and bureaucratic arrogance and stupidity play a big part in their management and control. Therefore, they simply contribute nothing to the mobility of the population. They are of no earthly value to anyone needing to find quickly a place where the family can lay their heads happily and safely.

Even in the communist countries, where all housing is publicly built and operated, state-owned housing is not much of a success. It involves more scandalous mismanagement, rank favoritism, discrimination, under-the-table bribery and official corruption in the communist lands than we have yet seen in America, according to most foreign observers. The only thing about communist public housing that seems to be good is that it is quite affordable because it is untaxed and highly subsidized.

Since a voluntarily mobile society is essential to the successful operation of a free enterprise economy and society, we need much more privately built and operated rental housing, the management of which is not subject to the red tape restraints, discrimination and delays of bureaucrats.

The only way we are going to get any large new accumulation of rental housing built and managed by private enterprise is to provide incentives to builders and developers. Tax incentives have been made available for this, but they aren't enough. They don't really work.

What will work?

Only wiping out inflation and getting costs and interest rates down to levels that will make contractors and real estate people willing to borrow money and invest it in rental housing for ordinary people instead of in speculative luxury housing for the rich. The lack of an adequate supply of rental housing frustrates both industry and labor, and the more modestly people are circumstanced the more they are frustrated. When people have to shell out half of their take-home pay just for shelter and utilities the burden becomes almost unbearable and leads to extremes of anxiety and actual hardship.

But the cost goes far beyond economics. It's bad enough for respectable persons to have to live in shabby, dreary, crime-ridden neighborhoods because that's all they can find or afford. The frustration of this can lead to drug addiction and other moral letdowns. But what is worse is when young couples want to set up housekeeping and have a baby or two and can't find quarters they can afford or would risk trying to rear a child in. This often leads to embitterment or serves as an excuse for embarking on a life of cynical hedonism. Since the nation obviously has no need of a larger population at the moment, some people may believe it is not important that young couples don't create stable new households. But it *is* important! Western civilization, and indeed the society of most of the world, is based on monogamous marriage.

We only have to think about two undesirable current social phenomena in America to realize what a serious matter this is. One is the extraordinary spread of homosexuality, the other the astonishing spread of a hitherto little known venereal disease called herpes simplex, for which there appears to be no certain permanent cure. Millions of persons of all ages have contracted it in recent years. It is a favorite topic of frenzied discussion in the news media. One wag said recently that herpes is likely to make adultery too dangerous to be fashionable. That was wishful thinking. What herpes simplex is doing is creating a vast amount of misery, fear and neurotic behavior in our country.

Married couples who are faithful to each other and have satisfactory living quarters do not contract or spread herpes.

Lack of adequate, sanitary living quarters is conducive to a lot of other health problems. Tuberculosis, which was believed to have been conquered in the United States forty years ago, is spreading again. TB is a disease associated, for the most part, with poor living conditions and overcrowding. Some other infectious diseases also are again on the increase, very possibly because of overcrowded living quarters.

The economic consequences of the acute shortage of rental housing are every bit as serious as the social consequences. Industry flees the big cities partly because good workers cannot find affordable, safe living quarters near urban jobs. Many poor persons stay on welfare because if they are offered jobs they cannot find rental housing nearby their work and the time and money it takes to get to and from the job makes it seem not worthwhile. For industry, choosing a plant or an office site involves finding available housing for workers convenient to schools, hospitals, shopping centers and recreation facilities.

But the most significant economic consequence is that the shortfall in rental housing probably is the biggest single cause of the disastrous decline in disposable personal savings in our population because high rents and high mortgage payments eat up savings. It may be argued that the banks and other thrift institutions and the landlords that collect these high shelter payments reinvest them in industry, but that's quite a dubious proposition. The thrift institutions are more likely to plow the payments back into speculative real estate, office buildings and luxury housing than to invest them in industry.

What are the real causes of the acute shortage of affordable rental housing?

The subsidies for buying homes that Congress gave the veterans returning from World War II and the Korean War had a lot to do with it. Several million houses were built and sold under the GI subsidies and in the affluent 1950s and 1960s these houses appreciated steadily in value; pretty soon other people besides war veterans and their wives got the idea that buying a house was the best way to save. Then along came inflation and the appreciation in the prices of homes skyrocketed.

But at the same time, inflation made the cost of building homes also skyrocket and made interest rates go up so high that construction loans and mortgages became extremely difficult to obtain. Thus, the housing boom finally collapsed insofar as ordinary folk are concerned. It became an affair only for the well-to-do, or at least those with considerable savings.

That, of course, is common knowledge. On this subject, I am not telling readers anything they don't already know.

But what many persons may not realize is that there is another and perhaps more fundamental reason for our failure to build an adequate supply of affordable rental housing, and that this reason is an important clue to what really is wrong with our entire economy.

Recently a stock market arbitrage trader wrote a letter to *The New York Times* in answer to an editorial expressing concern about the way big business has been squandering money on huge mergers instead of investing capital in new plants and expanding production. The arbitrager said the trouble is that our tax system and our government's policies make it a lot more profitable and safe for big business to speculate in existing enterprises by the merger route than to invest in new enterprises and expand the economy.

A moment's reflection tells us that this is also the case in housing. Our whole cockeyed economic situation makes it much more profitable for investors and real estate people to speculate in new and existing luxury housing than to build a large number of affordable rental houses and apartments for ordinary people.

To shorten a long story, the housing mess in America got steadily worse in the 1970s. Inflation ran the prices of houses so high that by the last years of the Carter administration the dream of owning one's home had faded for all except the well-to-do, yet the supply of alternative rental housing was diminishing steadily. The rise in taxes, labor costs and heating expense resulting from the Arab oil embargos ran the operating costs of apartment buildings so high that the landlords resorted to converting their buildings from rental units to co-operative units on a huge scale, or to condominiums in order to make tenants buy them out and take over the rising costs.

For a while, there was a boom in some parts of the country in new luxury condominium projects, particularly in Florida and in other retirement areas.

For those who buy them and live in them, a co-operative or a condominium apartment can be a lovely deal—as long as its value keeps appreciating. In New York City in the late 1970s, it was not uncommon for a family to buy a co-op apartment from the landlord for twenty thousand dollars and sell it for seventy thousand two or three years later. The co-op market still is pretty good at this writing, but the bottom fell out of the luxury condominium market some time before the arrival of the recession of 1981–82, and those who had bought luxury condominiums often found themselves living in quarters that had become an expensive burden and were depreciating in market value instead of going up.

The market for new single-family luxury houses selling for seventy-five to more than a hundred and fifty thousand dollars continued to be pretty good throughout 1981 and 1982, but the demand was confined to those who could afford a big down payment and the "creative" mortgage financing deals with fantastic interest rates, and giving the lender an equity share in any future market appreciation of the property.

Although there seems to be a surprising number of persons (some of them doubtless members of the underground economy) who can afford this luxury housing, it is quite obvious that these fancy domiciles add no real economic or social values to the nation. They are pleasant enough for those who can afford them, but in economic and social terms, they are mere conspicuous consumption, like so many gaudy bordellos.

What the American people need now is several million units yearly of new affordable small houses and apartments that can be rented or purchased. New construction in 1982 approached one million units and very little of that was rental housing affordable to ordinary families. So the million units didn't make a dent in the housing shortage. They didn't come anywhere near keeping pace with the combination of pent-up demand, growing population and shrinking supply of housing caused by the demolition of slum properties that were no longer safe or habitable.

The acute housing mess is a matter of some personal dismay to me because the industry in which I have spent my working career, insurance, is in no small degree responsible for it. Of all the big financial institutions in the country, the insurance companies, particularly the big establishment mutual life companies, are in the best position to pitch in and solve the housing problem. If these giant companies had been run in the past by far-sighted, public spirited men, the present terrible housing mess never would have occurred. For the truth of the matter is that insurance companies have been looked to by the builders and real estate developers as a prime source of construction loans and long-term financing.

Instead of realizing and accepting the social and economic importance to the nation of an abundant supply of rental housing for all classes of the populace, the insurance industry investment managers have been greedy for the big profits they envisioned in huge office complexes, shopping centers and luxury housing projects. They discouraged developers from putting up housing for ordinary white-collar and blue-collar workers in the big cities or elsewhere. They showed little or no sense of true rational social or economic responsibility. It's not too late for the insurance companies to change their tune and take the lead in a national movement to encourage the building of large amounts of affordable rental housing by private enterprise, and they certainly ought to do so.

The life insurance companies have inhibited not only the building of housing but the entire economy in another and more serious way. I spoke earlier in this chapter about high rents due to the housing shortage being perhaps the biggest single cause of our current lamentably low rate of disposable personal savings. Another big cause of this failure to save adequately is the trickery employed by the life insurance establishment for almost a century and a half in getting people to buy vastly over-priced cash value, whole life insurance policies under the deliberately planted delusion that they were engaging in a sensible savings program.*

Heaven only knows how many billions of dollars have been diverted over the years from investment in productive enterprises into ill-gotten profits for life insurance company promoters and big establishment life company

---

*For a full explanation of this sham, see *How Your Life Insurance Policies Rob You*, by Arthur Milton, Citadel Press, New York, 1981.

insiders by the life companies' predatory policies. At the very least, policyholders' money that should have remained in their hands as disposable personal savings was locked into life insurance policies that often paid miserable returns for the money invested. But it has been worse than that; the policyholders were deliberately deceived into thinking their policies were gaining in value much faster than was the fact. They were not told the blunt truth that life insurance is protection, not a way to save, and they were sold inadequate protection in their prime years on the specious plea that the money they were paying in was going into sensible savings.

If people had been sold reasonably priced term life insurance protection instead of the costly cash value whole life policies for the past century and a half, they would have been able to put many additional billions of dollars into savings accounts and more profitable investments that would have helped industry and commerce.

Happily, this long overdue change in the life insurance business at last is starting. Some life insurance companies and many life insurance marketers and agents are selling term insurance protection in large amounts at reasonable prices and urging their customers to buy annuities or otherwise invest their disposable savings in ways that will help the economy as well as protect their own futures.

What it all comes down to is that sooner or later we must restore population mobility in America if our economic ills are to be cured, and that means we must find some way to recreate the abundant supply of rental housing the nation enjoyed before World War II.

This brings us back to what I talked about at the beginning of this book: the necessity to check inflation permanently and bring interest rates down to normal. That will take time, and since the struggle necessarily involves casualties such as lost jobs and other hardships, there will be constant efforts by politicians, labor leaders, social workers and others to elect officials who will give up the struggle against inflation and revert to reckless government spending to spread employment and welfare benefits. We need to be compassionate to the casualty victims, but we also owe it to our children and to ourselves to resist these efforts to revert to extravagance and irresponsibility with all the intelligence and determination we can muster. We need to support Ronald Reagan's basic philosophy even if many of us disagree with him about details.

As this book ends I wish you to remember John F. Kennedy's ringing admonition: "Ask not what your country can do for you; ask what you can do for your country."

The time is now to put partisan politics aside and support our president to preserve the principles that made our country so great. Then, the Free American Enterprise System shall remain a beacon for all the world to admire, and our nation will forever persevere of the people, for the people and by the people.

Conclusion

THE MIDTERM ELECTIONS of November, 1982, were in some ways like the elections of 1862 and 1864 when, in the middle of the Civil War, Abraham Lincoln had to stave off strong challenges at the polls by northern pacifists who wanted to halt the struggle and let the seceded states go their way and perpetuate the evil institution of slavery in the South.

When Ronald Reagan took office in the White House he started a war . . . a war against ultra-liberalism, a war against the give-away programs, a war against fraud in government, a war against everything we did wrong for thirty-five to forty years in these United States of America, and let me tell you something, whether he is in the White House for four years or eight years, he is not going to be able to right all the wrongs. But already I can tell you this: He has set the course the United States must sail for the next fifty years.

So the election of 1982 was to all intents and purposes a wartime election and we must remember that in every war there are casualties. I am not speaking of the political casualties; they don't count for much or deserve overmuch sympathy. I am speaking of the economic and social casualties: the unemployed, the people whose fortunes and hap-

210

piness have been blighted by crime, violence, drug abuse, official and social corruption and educational irresponsibility.

Unthinking persons falsely blame these casualties on Ronald Reagan. He is actually to blame for very few of them. No governmental policy ever succeeds one hundred percent and a few of the Reagan policies have failed so far and caused hardship, but unlike the shrill-voiced opposition politicians and the ultra-liberals in the populace, the majority of the voters were not fooled in the 1982 electoral campaign. To be sure, the Democrats gained a few more seats than normal for the opposition in a mid-term election in the House of Representatives and elected a few governors, but on the whole Ronald Reagan fared better than most presidents do in a mid-term hustings. The Republicans retained control of the Senate and analysis of the popular vote showed a protest margin of only 1 to 2 percent over those voting support for his policies. The analysts said the results might put some pressure on Federal Reserve Board Chairman Paul Volcker to ease credit a little and might strengthen the hands on Capitol Hill of the foes of the Reagan defense spending program. But the *Wall Street Journal* noted shrewdly in its leading story two days after the election that the basic Reagan attack on inflation and high interest rates was not threatened by the result at the polls because the Democrats had no constructive alternative program to offer.

The results rather underline a remark made to a UPI reporter by Herman Kahn, the magnetic but somewhat controversial wizard of the Hudson Institute research think tank. Kahn said that, like Franklin Delano Roosevelt, Ronald Reagan seems to be remarkably successful at winning the loyalties and respect of men and women of extremely diverse ideas, convictions, backgrounds and personalities and get them to work well together.

Ronald Reagan is a decent man and a sincere man and that is a lot more important in the White House than being remarkably gifted intellectually. Intellectuals can become too arrogant to be effective, and so can professional politicians who, comparatively early in their careers, succumb to the notion that a politician's first and most important duty is to get reelected and must not let anything really stand in the way of that.

So what Helene Von Damm told me about Ronald Reagan's concept of the citizen politician as opposed to the professional politician may be the most important thing to remember about his character and personality, and this may prove to be his greatest gift to the nation. The longer I live the more I distrust professional politicians, and the less value I attach to experience in public office. Indeed, I incline to the theory that we would be a lot better governed if we were governed entirely by amateurs, newcomers to politics and public administration.

The essence of Reagan's citizen politician philosophy is his determination to behave in office as if he were never going to run for office again. I believe he lived up to that philosophy as governor of California and has lived up to it in his first two years in the White House. That set me to thinking about how wonderful it would be if all or most politicians showed so much character. If Richard Nixon had adopted this citizen politician philosophy and stuck to it conscientiously, the nation would have been spared the Watergate scandal. Nixon would not have had to resign in disgrace, the careers of several of his top aides would not have ended in indictments and jail terms and the war in Vietnam might have ended a lot sooner with many lives saved.

Even those Americans who despise Richard Nixon admit he is intelligent and capable, but they say his whole personality is warped by a stultifying obsession with professionalism in politics, that he is a total political animal, not a citizen, and hardly a real human being. Of course, that's an extremist view of Nixon. Others among us see him in a far more charitable light as the victim of circumstances and events he didn't create.

But nearly all the things that went wrong during the Nixon-Ford and Carter administrations and many of the foreign policy blunders made during Lyndon Johnson's administration can be traced fairly accurately to arrogant political professionalism, the belief of the professional politician that what he considers good for himself has to be good for the people.

Very possibly, we should start reducing or eliminating professionalism in American politics. The first and most practical step would be to limit tenure in all elective offices, at least in all elective federal and state offices, to a single term and abolish all pensions for holders of elective offices, thus making a professional career in politics financially impractical for any man or woman. Then indeed, only those willing to be citizen politicians and make their major remunerative careers outside of politics could serve. They would have much less incentive in public office to consider their own careers ahead of the public welfare and the people's interests.

Reagan's finest example of his devotion to the ideal of the citizen politician may have been his handling of the air traffic controllers strike that started in August, 1981. The strike clearly was illegal and a plain defiance of the authority of the government. By firing the ten thousand controllers after giving them a chance to return to work, Reagan struck a blow for honest principle and for economic and social common sense that was a turning point in the history of public labor relations. Reagan's precedent was roundly condemned by organized labor officials, both at home and abroad, and he necessarily caused a curtailment of airline service that greatly inconvenienced both the public and business and cost the airlines and many other businesses untold millions in lost revenue.

The controllers strike was followed by a business recession that reduced labor's power to hit back at the president with other crippling strikes. Nevertheless, it is clear the unions of public workers got the message clearly that the man in the White House would not permit a continuance of the drift toward anarchy that tolerance of illegal strikes of government and public agency workers would lead to. There was a notable diminution in strike threats by police and fire department unions, sanitation workers and government office workers all across the land when it became apparent that Mr. Reagan was not going to give in and take the fired air traffic controllers back. And there were fewer teachers strikes in the autumn of 1982, and those that did occur were settled rather quickly because judges in some areas threatened to jail teachers who struck illegally and did not obey a court order to return to work.

The failure of state and local governments to adequately enforce perfectly valid laws forbidding strikes by public workers—the New York subway and bus strikes, for example—had become a growing scandal in the country in the past fifteen years or so. Hopefully, Reagan's firm action in the air traffic controllers strike has arrested this dangerous trend permanently.

Of course, it may be argued that Reagan isn't going to get the support of organized labor if he runs for reelection anyway so he wasn't risking much by his tough stand in the controllers strike. But the real question is not formal support of the union leaders; it is well known that these officials cannot deliver all the labor vote and often cannot even deliver a majority of it. What Reagan risked in breaking the controllers strike was antagonizing rank and file union workers and especially the rank and file of the unions of Civil Service and other public and quasi-public workers. That risk seemed considerable at the time but in the end the common sense of working Americans prevailed. The controllers themselves admitted as much; they were astonished at how little sympathy they got from the rank and file members of other unions and from working people in general for their illegal strike.

The controllers also were deeply surprised and chagrined at the way the airlines and other businesses, resort areas, hotels and motels and travel agencies, for example, who were hard hit financially by the strike, backed the president in his stand in spite of the contraction of their businesses. Obviously, they did so because they thought Reagan was right.

It is time for all the rest of us to show some of the same firm resolve and determination that Mr. Reagan demonstrated in dealing with the controllers strike. We must stop being soft on decadent and evil trends that are sapping our national vitality and crippling our national productivity and our willpower as a people. We must face up to reality and stop wringing our hands over our apparent weaknesses.

For example, why did we ever imagine that the overwhelming economic power we attained right after World War II, when Europe and Asia lay prostrate as a result of the war, would last forever and we could coast along at the top of the world without any formidable competition? We acted as if our affluence at that time would continue forever without our working for it. It was inevitable that Europe and Asia would recover and that we would again face stiff competition all over the world. By sticking our heads in the sand like ostriches, we invited severe competition from the recovering and emerging nations not only in global markets but in our home markets. And now we wring our hands about it all.

Recently I heard about a book that Professor Jack Felman of Stevens Tech in Hoboken, New Jersey, and Professor Gavin Lewis of the City University of New York are working on that bears on this subject. They contend that American industry has not really lost its technological edge, that we still are far ahead of the rest of the world in technology on a broad front. What has happened to us, they say, is that we have lost the ability to make our technological edge felt and make it work properly because we are reduced to confusion by clinging to an outmoded economic and social philosophy based on confrontation between labor and management, between business and government and between business and the academic and scientific world. Professors Felman and Gavin say we can't copy Japanese methods in general, but if we would follow their example of cooperation instead of confrontation and work together with good teamwork most of our problems would become solvable.

But to do what they suggest implies a great deal of change in our present attitudes and practices. For instance, we would have to stop being so hedonistic, quit diverting so much of our energies and our capital into such wasteful and non-productive enterprises as gambling casinos and racetracks, not let ourselves be so taken in extravagant fascination with the stupidities of television and with the large-scale extravagance of big-time professional and college spectator sports.

Such fripperies as rock music and electronic videogames are symptomatic of much of what is wrong in America. They should not be outlawed, but the astonishing preoccupation of the public with them is something to be concerned about. They have a vastly wasteful and distorting effect on both society and business. And it goes without saying that the amount of time and money we Americans waste on pornographic literature and films shouts out loud to the wide world that we are becoming a decadent and wasteful people.

Consumer credit card excesses, the unrestrained brazenness of recklessly exaggerated advertising claims and the raucous vulgarity of much broadcast advertising also bespeak the growth of a frenzied and frivolous climate of irresponsibility in much of our population.

Instead of frittering away our energies and our capital on vulgar vagaries, we ought to be concerned about righting the many things that have gone wrong in recent years— about the fact that the combination of high interest rates and inflation have brought most of the country's farmers to the edge of bankruptcy and rebellion and that, in time, could threaten our food supply. It could threaten starvation for much of the world, for America not only feeds Americans but much of the rest of the globe as well.

This farm problem is only one of those we need to solve, but it is a most serious and fundamental one. Some rich farmers draw huge crop support subsidies from the government and most farmers get some support payments, but in spite of these payments, and in spite of the fact that food prices are sky high, most farmers appear to be having a rough time. Somewhere on the long line from farm to the supermarket shelf, perhaps at many different stations on the route, there are foulups that are symptomatic of the national lapse into greed, sloth, stupidity and corruption.

It is universally conceded that the farmer is a victim of his own productivity. For the past sixty years, his production per manhour worked and per acre tilled has gone up miraculously and still is increasing so much it hardly seems possible that it can keep rising at such rates for the next fifty years.

Ronald Reagan isn't an expert in the complications of the problems we have to solve, but he has shown us convincingly the kind of mental attitude and moral stamina we all must display if the problems are to be solved.

He has demonstrated much more. He has demonstrated that the vigor, independence, sense of justice, courage, honesty and optimism that have marked the people of this nation since colonial times still are vibrantly alive in ordinary Americans.

And Ronald Reagan is a man of the common people, make no mistake about that. Only a handful of our presidents actually have come from humble circumstances; most came from fairly well-to-do families and somewhat aristocratic backgrounds, but Ronald Reagan is the son of a not very successful shoe salesman who had something of a drinking problem, so his early years saw a family struggle for existence in a small town in Illinois, a twentieth-century version of the kind of social and economic climate Abraham Lincoln grew up in. Young Reagan didn't have to do as much hard, physical labor as young Lincoln did and he had access to better educational opportunities. Times had changed in a hundred years; rural Illinois no longer was frontier country. Nevertheless, Reagan reached college age just as the Great Depression began in earnest, and working his way through little Eureka College was no cinch even though he was a pretty good football player. Small colleges did not give opulent athletic scholarships in those days.

When he graduated, he had to create a job for himself. He wasn't the first radio sportscaster in the land but the field was so new that young Reagan had to travel from town to town seeking to convince some station owner that broadcasts of football and baseball games could be exciting and attract an audience, and that a kid fresh out of a hick college could be entrusted with the task.

He did so well as a sportscaster that rather soon he made his way to Hollywood and became a successful actor. He also became active in the union movement and was a rather warm supporter of Franklin Delano Roosevelt's New Deal policies. It is probable that, consciously or subconsciously, he absorbed much of his concept of the citizen politician from Roosevelt. Because FDR was elected president four times and served longer than any other man in the White House, it may be difficult for younger Americans today to accept the fact that he was not a professional politician in the modern sense.

It's true that FDR served in the New York legislature when he was young, that he was assistant secretary of the Navy during World War I. And it is true that he was nominated for vice-president as the running mate of ex-Governor James M. Cox of Ohio in 1920. But he never was overfond of campaigning and always considered himself above the kind of unscrupulousness and ruthless vulgarity that marks most of today's professionals in politics. He was drafted to run for governor of New York in 1928 when Al Smith ran for president unsuccessfully.

FDR ran for president in 1932 because he had lost faith in Smith's ability to win and with his ability to cope with the Great Depression if by chance he did win. As president, he was what a popular book's title called him, a "Country Squire in the White House," a gentleman and a citizen rather than a cold-blooded, totally selfish and power-hungry professional.

The irony is that he attained the greatest power and greatest success of any president in our history, yet much of this greatness was thrust upon him by the rise of Adolf Hitler's Rome-Berlin Axis and the menace of Japanese aggression in the Pacific.

It is highly unlikely that he would have sought a third term or could have been elected again in 1940 if the rest of the world had not been at war and the United States threatened on both coasts.

As I pointed out in my interview with Helene Von Damm, Ronald Reagan discovered early on that FDR was well aware that, because of the grim situation created by the depression, Congress had given him and arrogated to itself unprecedentedly broad powers that posed a grave danger to the future of the nation if they should be abused.

FDR said this bluntly and frankly on more than one occasion. The nation was at war during the rest of Roosevelt's days and the White House needed these broad powers, but FDR looked on these new powers of the national government with the gravest misgivings.

He foresaw that under peacetime conditions they could lead to political, social and economic disaster for the nation because they could and probably would be abused by selfish and irresponsible professional politicians.

From the end of World War II on, Reagan saw FDR's fears on this score come true. He saw thirty-five years of growing and gross abuse of power by professional politicians playing down to the greedy and irresponsible elements of the population. He saw this abuse erode much of the accomplishments and ideals achieved by the hard toil, sober thrift and honesty of our forefathers in a hundred and fifty colonial years and our first one hundred and seventy years as a free and independent nation. Ironically, this erosion process accelerated in the four years following our bicentennial as a nation in 1976.

It was seeing this corrosive and degenerative process that turned Reagan away from the Democratic Party and made him eventually seek the governorship of California and the presidency. We should be mighty thankful that he did see the light early and devoted himself to bringing the whole disastrous slide to a halt. He did a great job for all of us by beating Jimmy Carter in 1980 and has done an excellent job in his first two years as president. Among those who disagree with that conclusion are many of the casualties of his war on inflation and high taxes, and those ideologues who believe in big government and big spending. His enemies also include the selfish, irresponsible professional politicians. But for those Americans, no matter what their background or education, who are ruled by common sense, intellectual honesty and practical idealism, his stubborn determination to finish the war against inflation and high taxes is overwhelmingly the right course.

In 1977, I published a book entitled *Will Inflation Destroy America?* On the opening page, I said, "Our most pressing task is to bring a permanent end to uncontrolled

inflation," and I added, "It can be done." But my conclud-
ing paragraphs in that book were rather gloomy. I wrote,
"The TV tube has made us a nation of watchers instead of
doers . . . the computer has eliminated much of the need
to think; instead we punch buttons . . ." and "the credit
card has made it easy to become financial cripples, irresponsible and often bankrupt."

Thanks to Ronald Reagan's leadership of our nation, I
feel a lot more hopeful now than I did then. At last we can
see the light at the end of the tunnel and we can envision at
no distant future the United States again becoming a
strong, virile and productive nation.

Thank you, President Reagan, for setting our sails back
on the right course for all the world to see and emulate.

God bless you, and God bless America.

AMERICA THE BEAUTIFUL
PATRIOTIC HYMN
(Mixed Voices)

KATHARINE LEE BATES

WILLIAM ARMS FISHER